NAVIGATING THE
HEALTHCARE
WORKFORCE
SHORTAGE

NAVIGATING THE
HEALTHCARE
WORKFORCE
SHORTAGE

How to Safeguard Your Organization's Most Important Asset

Tresha Moreland and Lori Wightman

ACHE Management Series

Your board, staff, or clients may also benefit from this book's insight. For information on quantity discounts, contact the Health Administration Press Marketing Manager at (312) 424-9450.

This publication is intended to provide accurate and authoritative information in regard to the subject matter covered. It is sold, or otherwise provided, with the understanding that the publisher is not engaged in rendering professional services. If professional advice or other expert assistance is required, the services of a competent professional should be sought.

The statements and opinions contained in this book are strictly those of the authors and do not represent the official positions of the American College of Healthcare Executives or the Foundation of the American College of Healthcare Executives.

26 25 24 23 22   5 4 3 2 1

Library of Congress Cataloging-in-Publication Data

Names: Moreland, Tresha, author. | Wightman, Lori, author.
Title: Navigating the healthcare workforce shortage : how to safeguard your organization's most
    important asset / Tresha Moreland and Lori Wightman.
Other titles: Management series (Ann Arbor, Mich.)
Description: Chicago, IL : Health Administration Press, [2022]. | Series: HAP/ACHE management series | Includes bibliographical references and index. | Summary: "This book provides simple, practical, and proven strategies for healthcare leaders to address one of the biggest workforce shortages in recent history. The ideas and plans presented are built on real-life examples of organizations that have successfully overcome their workforce challenges"— Provided by publisher.
Identifiers: LCCN 2021017874 (print) | LCCN 2021017875 (ebook) | ISBN 9781640552876 (paperback ; alk. paper) | ISBN 9781640552845 (epub) | ISBN 9781640552852 (mobi)
Subjects: MESH: Personnel Management—methods | Health Workforce
Classification: LCC RA971.35 (print) | LCC RA971.35 (ebook) | NLM W 80 | DDC 362.10683—dc23
LC record available at https://lccn.loc.gov/2021017874
LC ebook record available at https://lccn.loc.gov/2021017875

The paper used in this publication meets the minimum requirements of American National Standard for Information Sciences—Permanence of Paper for Printed Library Materials, ANSI Z39.48-1984. ⊗ ™

Acquisitions editor: Jennette McClain; Manuscript editor: Deborah Ring; Project manager: Andrew Baumann; Cover design: James Slate; Layout: Integra

Found an error or a typo? We want to know! Please email it to hapbooks@ache.org, mentioning the book's title and putting "Book Error" in the subject line.

For photocopying and copyright information, please contact Copyright Clearance Center at www.copyright.com or at (978) 750-8400.

Health Administration Press
A division of the Foundation of the American
    College of Healthcare Executives
300 S. Riverside Plaza, Suite 1900
Chicago, IL 60606-6698
(312) 424-2800

*This book is dedicated to the memory of someone very close—
Lisa, who always believed in me and cheered me on. Her forever
words of encouragement and my faith have become an undercurrent
for determination, resilience, and how this book was completed.
In Lisa's words: "No challenge gets in the way of doing
what you think is right."*
—Tresha Moreland

*This book is dedicated to my late husband, Allen, who inspired me
and encouraged me throughout my career. His strength, perseverance,
and love of people influenced me as a leader. I attribute much of my
success to his role modeling and coaching.*
—Lori Wightman

Contents

Preface

THIS BOOK PROVIDES a jumping-off point for creative thinking about how to use existing resources to narrow the workforce shortage in your healthcare organization. It offers practical strategies for healthcare executives navigating one of the biggest workforce shortages of our time. Information is drawn straight from the field and backed by real-life examples of how healthcare organizations are addressing workforce supply challenges. Times have changed, and so has the talent we seek to fill our vacancies.

The successful use of this book will require three things:

1. Openness to new ideas
2. Courage to question the status quo
3. Curiosity to experiment, monitor, and adjust practices

This mindset will help you avoid the trap of making incorrect assumptions about your organization. For example, if your eyes tend to glaze over when talking about organizational culture, you may be tempted to skip that chapter. However, culture may be the very thing that is preventing your organization from attracting and retaining talent and thereby easing your workforce shortage. Executives who have an open mind, courage to question the status quo, and curiosity stand a better chance of dodging such pitfalls.

To get the most out of this book, consider the following recommendations:

- Take a step back and put aside "the way we do it here." What would be possible if your organization did something different to fill even one more vacancy or retain one more employee?

- Consider setting up a cross-functional team to model the mindset described above. Have the team evaluate your organization against the six key levers described in this book. Make it safe for them to ask questions, challenge the status quo, raise concerns, and make recommendations. From the executive level, you may feel it's safe to speak up. But is it safe for all those who may have valuable suggestions for your organization's recruitment and retention efforts?

- Don't just talk about it. Have you sat in meetings in which hours go by with lots of debate and discussion, yet nothing happens? Plan, act, and do. Time is wasting away!

- Make an authentic effort to enhance your ability to impact workforce shortages. It should not be a part of political positioning, power building, or pet projects. If you really want to attract and retain employees, start by being authentic throughout the process.

Acknowledgments

My sincerest appreciation for Kathleen Klawitter, my visionary coach, and Libby Gill's executive coaching group and endless writing sprints, which motivated me to pursue my professional dreams.

—*Tresha Moreland*

I would like to acknowledge my executive coach, Pat Barlow, and my longtime mentor, Gay Landstrom, for their many years of guidance and encouragement.

—*Lori Wightman*

Introduction

THE PERFECT HEALTHCARE storm is here, and it threatens to become more intense before it subsides. The driving winds of environmental, demographic, and market conditions are fueling the storm for healthcare systems, providers, and clinics across the United States. The situation has been exacerbated by the unexpected arrival of maximum-strength winds in the form of COVID-19, economic volatility, and civil unrest.

If healthcare leaders were not thinking about the future of healthcare and the significant challenges confronting the industry before 2020, they may have been shocked by the devastating effects of the multiple global crises we face today. The challenges facing the healthcare industry are many. To successfully navigate these challenges, we must identify and understand them, not duck and cover.

Let's break the challenges into specific, manageable categories.

THE "NEW NORMAL"

The pace of change in healthcare was fast before 2020, but the pandemic has taken things to an unprecedented level. Healthcare is experiencing rapid cycle changes; shifting stewardship of critical resources such as money, personal protective equipment (PPE), and the workforce; regulatory changes; changes in public perceptions; and shifts in healthcare services. It is not unusual to feel as if you are reacting hour by hour, if not minute by minute. You can no longer count on a policy to stand the test of time. Creative thinking is now a requirement for survival.

THE AGING UNITED STATES POPULATION

The aging US population is a key concern for policymakers, health system CEOs, and every American. According to Kaiser Health News, "Within 10 years, all of the nation's 74 million baby boomers will be 65 or older. The most senior among them will be on the cusp of 85."[1] In light of this significant growth, healthcare leaders must prepare their organizations to care for an ever-increasing Medicare population—a population that has the highest rates of chronic disease and the highest utilization of hospital and long-term care services.

MEDICARE INSOLVENCY AND SCARCE COVERAGE OF THE COST OF CARE

In 2020, the Medicare Trustees projected that the Hospital Insurance Trust Fund, which finances the Medicare program, will become insolvent by 2026 in the absence of change. This budget deficit is the result of rapid increases in the number of Americans over age 65 and declining numbers of workers paying into the Trust Fund. Regulatory changes, such as the repeal of the excise tax for high-cost employer-sponsored health plans (known as the "Cadillac tax"), have also contributed to the shortfall.

The threat of Medicare insolvency is not new. However, many are wondering how COVID-19 will impact the overall picture. Amid the volatility of the pandemic and the economic and regulatory climate, however, it is impossible to project any specific impact at the time of this writing.

Nevertheless, we can expect that the ongoing pandemic and economic upheaval will cause millions of people to become unemployed, affecting Medicare revenues and accelerating Medicare's insolvency. In September 2020, the Congressional Budget Office projected that the Hospital Insurance Trust Fund will become insolvent by 2024—two years earlier than originally forecast. The US Congress faces a heavy lift in revisiting policies to buoy the system. Healthcare executives are best suited to keep an eye on what promises to be a moving target.

Even if Medicare becomes solvent, even temporarily, existing coverage does not fully cover the cost of care. As a result, healthcare systems are forced to find ways to reduce the cost of care—in addition to balancing increasing consumer expectations, such as care-at-any-cost or hotel-like amenities. Healthcare executives understand that the vast majority of Americans do not understand how healthcare gets paid or what is causing the rising cost of care.

WORKFORCE SHORTAGES

To maintain exceptional care into the future, organizations in the United States need to hire an estimated 2.3 million new healthcare workers by 2025. The pandemic and economic instability, layered atop an already overburdened healthcare system, make workforce issues all the more complex. We must address critical questions, such as what new skill(s) tomorrow's healthcare will need, and where we will find or create talent. The following are just a few of the issues that arose during the pandemic that must be addressed:

- **Workers must be convinced that healthcare is a meaningful, safe career choice with potential for growth.** Healthcare organizations must find ways to help employees answer the question "Do I really want to work in healthcare?" Healthcare professionals are leaving the field with heavy burnout, moral distress, and the feeling that "this is not what I signed up for." The pandemic made visible to the public how difficult and emotionally draining the profession can be. As a result, it has become even more difficult to recruit healthcare professionals amid concerns about the safety of workers and their families.

- **Employees are facing competing home care demands.** Increasing demands at home are forcing healthcare workers to reduce their hours or stop working altogether to provide childcare or manage schooling.

- **Employees are leaving their current employers.** Healthcare workers who are near retirement age are opting for early retirement. Many are fatigued and have been personally affected by the COVID-19 pandemic in some way. In addition, many experienced caregivers are leaving their employers to take advantage of lucrative travel assignments to bolster their income.

- **Remote work presents new challenges.** Before the pandemic, many organizations were hesitant to allow employees to work from home. The pandemic forced the issue, however, and employers had to respond quickly, whether they were ready or not. Technology, cybersecurity, remote productivity, and effective management of remote teams are all daunting challenges that healthcare organizations must address.

COVID-19 MAGNIFIER: A NEW REALITY

As we celebrated the new year on January 1, 2020, we had no idea that we were about to confront a global pandemic that would shine a light on the healthcare industry's vulnerabilities. As if it were not daunting enough to face with the challenges outlined here, the pandemic placed a sudden strain on systems and healthcare professionals throughout the nation and the world.

(continued)

(continued from previous page)

At the urging of the White House Coronavirus Task Force and industry authorities, elective procedures and surgeries were put on hold to allow treatment of the sudden influx of COVID-19 patients and to preserve desperately needed medical supplies. The pause lasted for more than a month, causing a significant financial strain on healthcare systems.

The global crisis magnified weaknesses in the supply chains for medical supplies, hospital bed availability, and a shortage of ventilators. On the nightly news, we saw one healthcare worker after another in tears, concerned about the safety of themselves and their families because they lacked adequate PPE. The strain of states competing against one another for essential supplies became public. We also saw the nation rally around healthcare workers, with volunteers putting in countless hours to create handmade masks.

The pandemic did not resolve our workforce shortages. While the crisis and the lack of supplies understandably became the focus of many discussions, the shortage of skilled healthcare workers remained a persistent undercurrent. Reliance on expensive agency staff became necessary despite cost containment initiatives the prior year.

To cope with the significant reduction in revenue and the increased cost of labor and supplies, furloughs, layoffs, and pay cuts became a reality. Employee concerns about their safety, job security, and shortages of essential supplies (e.g., toilet paper, sanitizer, PPE, food) sent many healthcare systems right back to square one with respect to employee morale and engagement.

—*Tresha Moreland and Lori Wightman*

WHAT DOES ALL OF THIS MEAN FOR THE HEALTHCARE SYSTEM?

All of these driving winds point to a perfect storm that is far more dire than what we can see on our immediate horizon. In the future, healthcare organizations will be required to care for more people who have acute and chronic conditions. Some of those medical conditions may have emerged during the pandemic as people put off seeking care. These same healthcare organizations can expect to receive reduced reimbursements, coupled with declining patient volumes, and they will be forced to rely on a much smaller work-force to deliver complex care to more patients than ever before.

The debate rages on about how to solve the multiple crises that healthcare organizations face. Solving the workforce shortage and other healthcare challenges could take years, if not a whole genera-tion. Waiting for policymakers or legislation to solve our problems is not an option. Patients need care right now. The labor pool, reimbursements, and margins are shrinking. We must navigate the crisis with the resources we have available to us today.

There are countless examples of how health organizations are doing just that—using the resources and tools they have avail-able to navigate the workforce shortage. If we think of the health-care organization as a machine, those resources and tools are the "levers" that can be pulled to activate a specific part of the machine to achieve a desired outcome. This book is organized around six key levers that healthcare executives can pull or activate to address the workforce shortage, with real-life examples of each lever.

KEY LEVER 1: BUILDING ORGANIZATIONAL RESILIENCE—HOW'S YOUR BOAT HOLDING UP?

A healthcare crisis has been brewing for some time. But the COVID-19 pandemic ripped off the bandage and exposed the extent of the change that is needed. Once a crisis hits, it is too late to prepare your organization for survival. This section outlines ten steps that organizations can take to build strength and resilience. The goal is not just to be ready for change, but to successfully navigate challenges, abrupt shifts in direction, and crises. This section will discuss the value of "pre-work." If you are a leader who felt sideswiped by the pandemic, chapter 1 is for you.

We will consider what a resilient workforce looks like, how to leverage rather than burn relationships, and what communication techniques will help you build resilience. We will also dive into how leadership and workforce development come into play.

In this section, we will also cover technology platforms that can be used to adapt to our ever-changing world. Emergency management, financial stewardship, safety, and quality services are discussed in this section. The culture of innovation is also relevant for our reality; this section will outline the steps organizations need to take to develop a culture of innovation.

These areas may seem like priorities that organizations would have had in place before the pandemic. However, the crisis has given us a new lens through which to examine our priorities. It even shifted the focus of this book: When we began writing, we started down a pre-COVID-19 path; the global crisis, however, made clear that we needed to rethink the entire organization of this book. The sheer demand for healthcare services and the continuing strain on our workforce require that we adjust our priorities to ensure we emerge from the crisis, ahead of the workforce shortage storm.

KEY LEVER 2: CREATING A CULTURE BRAND AND POSITIONING YOUR ORGANIZATION COMPETITIVELY

Shaping organizational culture is not for the faint of heart, nor should it be taken for granted. In this section, we will explore what happens to culture when we are intentional rather than passive.

You will learn how to assess and influence organizational culture. If that's not enough, blending cultures through mergers and acquisitions is also on the menu in this section.

Leadership engagement is where the rubber meets the road in influencing culture. We will see how an engaged leader can be the single most effective or destructive force in forming a healthy workplace culture. This section also explores the art of storytelling and how to leverage it to connect the hearts and minds of employees to the organization's mission, vision, and objectives.

KEY LEVER 3: RETAINING EMPLOYEES—BECAUSE KEEPING PEOPLE MATTERS

Let's make the work environment matter to our employees. That means we must find ways to enhance the employee experience. This section will explore the difference between engagement and experience and guide you through the employee experience journey. Don't have deep budgetary resources to reward employees? That's alright—as we will show, it's the small things that matter.

This section will also explore ways to create a good employee experience. We will cover how to encourage personal growth to help employees rise above challenges such as stress and burnout. We will also discuss how to quantify turnover costs, use prevention techniques, respond rapidly to resignations, and leverage total rewards.

KEY LEVER 4: POWERING VALUE THROUGH ORGANIZATIONAL EFFECTIVENESS

If you are among the many organizations that struggle to move the needle on key objectives, that may mean there is misalignment afoot. Alignment is achieved when the organization is in the right place, at the right time, with the right set of capabilities to meet growing market demand. It means the organization is heading in the right direction, with little internal friction hindering rapid and effective execution. This section will cover how to test your organization's strategic alignment, how to achieve alignment, and how to realign organizational focus.

The pressures and speed of reaction in a crisis can cause drift—away from the organization's mission, vision, and values. Leaders need to talk about alignment with mission, vision, and values daily when organizations are under pressure. A discernment process will help prevent emotional drain when confronted with constant crisis. You can also connect the dots for the employees.

In addition to alignment, another force that can derail organizational success in navigating a crisis is the collective bargaining situation. Labor unions are quick to claim that a short-sided approach to solving the workforce shortage is to cut executive compensation and pay higher wages to covered employees. But we know that higher pay does not magically produce a skilled workforce, much less make people want to stay.

This section will go into how today's industry challenges are putting healthcare executives in a bind between required changes and bargaining unit resistance. We will explore how to strategize for collective bargaining and put accounting to good use in quantifying the contract as a whole, as well as each proposal.

KEY LEVER 5: LEVERAGING RECRUITMENT IN A DISRUPTED WORLD

Struggles with increasing turnover and retirement make recruitment an essential strategy for navigating the workforce shortage. But the "post and pray" method of recruitment is no longer effective. To examine leveraging recruitment in more effective ways, we will consider it in two parts: internal and external strategies. Each plays a critical role in the bigger picture of attracting hard-to-recruit talent. We will explore which numbers are important to know, how to align for a productive recruitment team, and why cross-functional collaboration is important. We will also look at how organizations are tapping into their own internal talent pools to fill gaps.

Many external recruitment strategies are available to get your organization's brand in front of viable candidates. We will look at how to tap into unique and diverse talent pools, how to maximize technology and social media, and how to engage the community and build partnerships.

While healthcare systems are busily recruiting people, travel agencies and competitors are working just as hard to lure your existing workforce away. We will discuss ways to deal with competing forces that threaten to take away your talent. Further, we will explore why current employees should be part of the recruitment process and why an authentic caring culture matters more than ever.

KEY LEVER 6: PREPARING FOR THE FUTURE OF WORK

The future of the healthcare industry seems foggy and tumultuous at times. Staring at the hood of our vehicle while driving prevents us from seeing what's coming down the road, particularly in difficult and stormy conditions. We need to understand how our rapidly shifting world affects the healthcare workforce so we can plan effectively. In this section, we will look at generational, work model, and technology shifts that impact our workplaces so that we can plan for the future.

This section will also discuss how to pull the future into the present through workforce planning. You will learn how to prepare for the unexpected. This section will dive into workforce optimization techniques as well as how to use people analytics to drive change.

Fellow navigators—let's begin our journey together.

NOTE

1. Graham, J. 2020. "What the 2020s Have in Store for Aging Boomers." Kaiser Health News. Published January 16. https://khn.org/news/what-the-2020s-have-in-store-for-aging-boomers/.

Building Organizational Resilience—How's Your Boat Holding Up?

IMAGINE SAILING ON the open sea. A soft breeze caresses the sails, the smell of sea salt wafts through the air, and the seagulls are squawking playfully. Suddenly, however, a storm approaches. The breeze quickly becomes a strong gust. The sound of the seagulls is replaced with rumbling thunder as lightning cracks through the dark and menacing sky.

Your boat begins to creak and moan under the strain of the crashing waves, but it holds strong. The sails are tough enough to withstand the pressure, and you adjust them to accommodate the shifting gale-force winds.

That is what resilience looks like. Resilience is the ability to bend or shift under pressure but not break. Organizational resilience is much more than a one-time training event that you cross off your checklist. It is the ability to anticipate crises and respond effectively to disruptions, even when they are unexpected and severe.

Once a crisis hits, it's too late to prepare your organization for survival. When a crisis hits an unprepared organization, it exposes the leadership and its practices as unprepared as well. An unprepared organization may struggle with communication, sending mixed or conflicting messages. Processes that once worked may break under the strain of gale-force winds. Employees may no longer have confidence that the organization is a safe place to be. They may stay put during an economic downturn, but at the next opportunity, they will leave the organization for greater security. The onslaught of the COVID-19 storm no doubt highlighted for many leaders the need to build a more resilient organization and workforce. Let's dive into how you can develop a more resilient organization.

CHAPTER 1

The Value of Pre-work: Ten Steps to Develop a Resilient Organization

WHEN A CRISIS strikes, it's too late to develop a plan. The speed of authentic and organized response is what employees need to see to have confidence in leadership during a crisis. This chapter outlines a ten-step process that will help prepare your organization and build the strength and resilience necessary to successfully navigate challenges, abrupt shifts in direction, and crises. A detailed Pre-work Checklist can be found in appendix A.

STEP 1: DO YOUR PERSONAL "PRE-WORK"

It is hard to lead teams and organizations effectively when you are fatigued, burned out, anxious, or fearful. We hire smart people, and they can see through our scripts and branding messages. Employees observe, listen, and compare notes. The ability to manage your own fear and anxiety and to muster courage is critical during a crisis.

It is also important to maintain your own health of mind, body, and spirit . . . all the time. You must be centered and lead with a clear mind and heart.

STEP 2: DEVELOP A RESILIENT WORKFORCE

Developing a resilient workforce is at the core of navigating a crisis or stepping up your attraction and retention processes. This work can be viewed through three lenses: employees, leaders, and mission and values.

Employees

The global crisis has shaken employee engagement. Surveys show that employee engagement across the board took a roller-coaster ride throughout the pandemic. There was a temporary uptick in engagement as people started working from home—except among essential workers, who did not feel safe. Then there was the uncertainty of watching friends and family get furloughed or lose their jobs altogether, causing employee engagement to take a dive. On top of all of this, employees were scared and confused about the safety recommendations concerning COVID-19.

Employee engagement is not about a survey score. It's about the underlying culture. A strong culture will support employee resilience. Building a resilient culture takes more than a one-time leadership training event. It requires ongoing nurturing and support of all who work in the organization. A supportive culture will encourage and develop resilient employees.

Resilient employees do things differently than others. They have a strong support system. They often can manage stress and burnout before they become a problem. Resilient employees have the passion and perseverance to run a marathon, rather than just a sprint. They have the mental toughness and flexibility to bounce back from difficult situations or setbacks. They will resist getting involved in unnecessary drama or engaging with negative people who drag them down. These employees are the organization's rock during times of difficulty.

Leaders

Are your leaders aligned with the organization's mission and values? The pandemic has revealed some essential truths about whether people in leadership positions lead with their head, or authentically with their heart. The days of "command and control," "leading by lip service," and self-centeredness are over. Employees see through empty PR statements and clearly observe leaders' actions as the center of their truth. The adage "actions speak louder than your words" is at the core of building or losing trust.

Even if leaders have lost ground with employee engagement, it's not too late to reenergize your workplace. But leaders must be willing to engage themselves and regenerate above and beyond their own crisis fatigue. Leaders must envision a better day and commit to a better way.

Leaders, like employees, have been deeply affected by the COVID-19 crisis. It is important for leaders to balance crisis with resilience, reflection, and support, so that they can show up with courage and in alignment with the organization's mission, vision, and values.

Mission and Values

Hiring in alignment with your mission and values is critical. Granted, doing so can be difficult, and it is often overlooked in favor of filling a vacancy quickly. But, more often than not, we have personally observed that engaging in convenience hiring over mission and values alignment results in turnover. This creates a perpetual tailspin of vacancies, low morale, and continuous pressure on leaders trying to run their operations, as well as on employees who provide the initial new employee training.

Savvy leaders will resist convenience hiring and take the time to hire individuals who are aligned with the organization's mission and values. Those are the employees who will support organizational direction and may just stick around for a while.

STEP 3: DEVELOP AUTHENTIC RELATIONSHIPS

There is a difference between authentic relationships and cliques. A clique is a small group of people who have interests or circumstances in common and spend time together. But they do not let others join their group easily. They may even work to ostracize talented people who are seen as different or a threat to their status or personal agenda. Cliques can be harmful in the workplace, and they work against the organization's ability to attract and retain talent, embrace diversity, and achieve overall organizational objectives.

A great deal of work has been done on the development of meaningful relationships and how doing so can positively influence culture and the communities around us. Mary Koloroutis and David Abelson, for instance, advance a framework of *relationship-based care*, which is a practical model that empowers leaders and employees to put relationships first.[1] It is a model for culture transformation that improves safety, quality, and patient and staff satisfaction by improving every relationship within the organization. This framework comprises three relationships:

1. Relationship with self
2. Relationship with colleagues
3. Relationship with patients and families

Whether or not your organization uses the relationship-based care model, the focus on these three key relationships is vital. Cover all your bases in the development of meaningful relationships.

Authentic relationships are based on trust. Trust forms when people feel safe in sharing their ideas and thoughts and do not fear being judged unfairly. Sit back and observe your team in earnest. What are some signs of authentic relationships? Employees ask questions in a way that builds positive energy and support. Labels, biases, and assumptions are checked at the door. People listen with their full attention, rather than focusing on emails and smartphones. Relationships are formed with the right intent: Is the intent purely transactional, or is there a genuine desire to be of value to the other person? Keys to evaluating your relationship-building level for several crucial stakeholder groups—employees, leaders, customers, and partners—are presented in exhibit 1.1.

While this seems elementary, we have observed even at senior levels the formation of cliques rather than authentic relationships. Cliques or authentic relationship behaviors can make or break leadership credibility in the crucial stakeholder's eyes. Assume that what happens in the board room does not always stay in the board room.

Exhibit 1.1 Keys to Evaluating Your Relationship-Building Level for Crucial Stakeholders

Employees
- Do your employees know and trust the organization's leadership *before* a crisis occurs?
- Are there divisions between departments or workgroups?
- Does the organization have a cultural expectation of teamwork, care, and compassion for colleagues?
- Do employees recognize and feel comfortable speaking to all levels of leadership in the organization?

Leaders
- Do your leaders embrace the importance of trust and respect?
- Do your leaders work hard at developing healthy working relationships?
- Do your leaders have a "one for all" approach and no "turf" building?
- Do your leaders possess grace and assume good intentions?

Customers
- Is it clear who the organization's customers are?
  - Who are the internal customers?
  - Who are the external customers?

(continued)

(continued from previous page)

- Are employed or affiliated physicians treated as customers?
- Do your relationships with patients and families go beyond chasing patient experience survey scores?
  - Do you meet their "hotel" expectations, or are you just a lifeline to the patient?
  - How did you manage the impact of "no visitors" during the pandemic?
  - How is your relationship with the community (or communities) you serve?
  - Does the community value and respect its community hospital and physician practices?
  - Does the community understand and value quality healthcare?
  - Does the organization engage in the community?

Partners
- How have you been developing partnerships with government officials? Advocacy work can help government officials understand healthcare and the challenges we face.
- Do you view vendors and representatives of supply companies as partners?
- How are your organization's relationships with manufacturers that supply products you use to serve patients?
- How are your relationships with other healthcare organizations?

COVID-19 MAGNIFIER: TECHNOLOGY BOOSTS PERSONAL CONNECTION

Technology enabled us to stay connected to one another during the pandemic, even if it was not the same as sitting across the table from a colleague.

Technology was used during the pandemic to increase the visibility of leadership through virtual town halls, meetings, and participation in clinical or safety rounds. This visibility to physicians and frontline caregivers was

(continued)

(continued from previous page)

vital to authentically communicate and create connection. COVID-19 safety measures included the restriction or elimination of visitors to hospitalized patients. Technology helped caregivers connect patients with their families. A virtual connection was better than no connection at all. Technology also helped caregivers monitor patients behind the closed doors of isolation rooms. Sometimes the technology was simple, such as baby monitors, while other times it was more elaborate, allowing visualization of the patient as well as two-way communication.

The pandemic forced a large portion of our workforce into their homes to conduct their work. Leaders and their teams quickly adapted to virtual meetings, training, and communication forums. While face-to-face interaction was sorely missed, we learned that we could be productive using virtual forums. However, virtual meetings taught us that we must be concise, offer time for informal interactions using chat functions, and be courageous and authentic. Enabling the video function during virtual meetings allows people to get a close-up view of you—to see your expressions and smile. Additionally, allowing people to peek into your personal space on video calls shows a side of you that colleagues would not normally have a chance to see. This authenticity creates connections.

Regardless of whether and when we return to office life, we have learned how to use technology to keep us connected.

—Lori Wightman

STEP 4: COMMUNICATE STRATEGICALLY AND EFFECTIVELY

Even if an organization has a well-thought-out emergency management plan, a communication strategy that is ill-conceived or an executive who sends the wrong message to employees can damage the organization's reputation and credibility. Poor communication can undermine any gains made in engagement before a crisis. A well-designed and well-executed communication strategy runs deep, wide, early, and often. It is timely, truthful, consistent, and coordinated.

We have seen leaders damage their credibility by delivering messages to team members that were not accurate or truthful. Underestimating how much people know or understand and then delivering inaccurate messages for any reason is a mistake. It is a fast way to undermine leadership reputation, employee trust, and engagement. Authenticity and truthfulness are essential qualities of any effective communication, and much more so during a crisis.

The pathways of effective communication are well worn. Communication must get to each employee—particularly those on the front lines, who are facing your customers. It is better for messages to be delivered to employees before they hear them on the evening news. Doing so signals to employees that you care enough to let them know about organizational news first and allows them to ask questions.

Visibility of leadership is the norm and may involve frequent forums, town hall meetings, and rounding. Leaders should be regularly engaged in visibility practices before a crisis happens. If leaders only show up on the front lines to deliver a message during a crisis, employees will learn to fear seeing the organization's leaders in the first place.

STEP 5: DEVELOP LEADERS AT ALL LEVELS OF THE ORGANIZATION

When it comes to leadership development, some organizations make the common mistake of starting at the top and then stopping. They may give in to the temptation to eliminate training as part of a cost-containment strategy. Or, organizations may go through great effort for a once- or twice-a-year leadership development event and then fail to ensure that the training is cascaded or applied to day-to-day activities. Here are some tips to ensure a prepared and resilient organization:

- Don't save training only for executives—frontline leaders are the ones putting strategy into action.
- Offer engaging annual (or more frequent) safety training and drills—don't blow it off!
- Cross-train employees and develop methods to deploy training throughout the organization so that all employees understand expectations.
- Recommend or sponsor leaders for new leadership roles during a crisis; bring leaders alongside you so that they gain exposure to different leadership work.
- Use low-cost techniques such as coaching and mentorship to support and develop leaders and set expectations for self-development and personal investment in growth.
- Build a portfolio of virtual learning opportunities available at all times and updated at sufficient intervals.

STEP 6: INVEST IN TECHNOLOGY PLATFORMS THAT CAN ADAPT QUICKLY

At the beginning of 2020, who could have foreseen the demand and government support for telehealth? Healthcare organizations are fortunate that the government lifted legislative constraints to enable healthcare systems to expand their use of telehealth technology. In addition, technology became instrumental to our ability to engage and develop remote workforces. Technology also allowed us to adapt by recruiting talent using virtual platforms. SCL Health is a not-for-profit Catholic healthcare system based in Broomfield, Colorado, with hospitals and clinics located in Kansas, Colorado, and Montana. The system has a physician network made up of primary care and specialty physicians. While telehealth visits were offered before the COVID-19 pandemic, physicians and patients generally relied on in-person office visits. Often clinics reported telehealth visits in the single digits. In February 2020, SCL Health's Denver-area clinics reported just 54 telehealth visits. By March 2020, however, more than 5,000 telehealth clinic visits were conducted. The physicians and their teams quickly pivoted to a telehealth strategy to provide care to patients quarantined at home.

STEP 7: REFRESH YOUR EMERGENCY MANAGEMENT TRAINING AND TEAM

Many healthcare systems had emergency management training programs in place before the COVID-19 pandemic. After all, regulatory bodies such as The Joint Commission require it. Most plans cover scenarios such as natural disasters (e.g., floods, earthquakes, hurricanes), power outages, and active shooters. How well did these emergency management training programs do at the onset of the COVID-19 pandemic? The following recommendations will help you recheck and refresh your emergency management policies and programs.

- A response structure must be created *in advance* of a crisis.
- Leaders at all levels should be trained regularly on emergency management principles and roles.

- In-house emergency management experts should provide direction and on-the-spot training during a crisis (e.g., a chief nursing officer as the system incident commander with an emergency management leader as the deputy incident commander).
- Drills must be taken seriously by all levels of leadership. If drills are stale and poorly attended, it's time to shake things up and make them fresh, real, and top of mind for everyone.
- Periodic scenario planning should be conducted to ensure that emergency management procedures account for events that have not been practiced (e.g., civil unrest, additional virus outbreaks).
- All levels of leadership need to engage in training (such as FEMA courses) to be able to respond in an aligned, effective manner. If nothing else, leaders must understand the response structure and activities. We have seen a number of executives who never took FEMA courses or formal training and struggled to understand their role during the COVID-19 pandemic response. A crisis is not a good time to train.
- In addition to emergency management plans, the organization needs to have multiple plans that address different levels of patient volume surge.
- Forget competition for the moment—healthcare systems, hospitals, medical groups, and their leaders need to come together to plan for the benefit of the communities they serve.

STEP 8: EVALUATE FINANCIAL STEWARDSHIP

While financial strain on the healthcare industry is nothing new, the sudden downturn spurred by the pandemic, coming after a booming economy, took many by surprise. Having a strong, disciplined regime for financial alerts will enable organizations to better deal with economic downturn when the cost of labor continues to go up. There are many ways to improve margins without reducing staff and risking outcomes. Here are a few questions you can ask to evaluate your position with respect to the workforce:

- Is the organization good at flexing to service demand?
- No margin, no mission: Do employees at all levels of the organization understand financial stewardship and their part in it? Remember, clinicians will embrace stewardship when you connect the dots—they need to understand how an initiative improves care or promotes safety. Clinicians like to be "good stewards," too—not "save money."
- Do you have a workforce optimization strategy? If so, is it focused on reducing costs rather than hours?
- Does your organization have a financial stewardship position in place *before* a crisis?

STEP 9: MAINTAIN SAFE AND HIGH-QUALITY SERVICES

Maintaining safe and high-quality services regardless of what is going on around us is critical in healthcare. During the pandemic, people naturally became fearful about entering hospitals because of COVID-19 concerns. Having a strong reputation for quality of care before a crisis will help soothe patient concerns and continue to attract a strong workforce.

Developing the skill and expertise required to deliver a high level of care before a crisis occurs prepares care teams to perform at an effective level during a crisis (e.g., intensive care units during the COVID-19 crisis).

Cross-training is vital for organizations to be resilient and responsive to crisis situations. This includes nontraditional cross-training, too. An example of nontraditional cross-training is utilizing business office staff to support patient care. How can you prepare business office and clinical staff for this type of scenario ahead of time? You can prepare employees' mindset in the event of a crisis by communicating frequently, by letting them know that they may be asked to support patient care, and by promoting agility, flexibility, and teamwork. For instance, prepare position descriptions that include needed competencies and training modules in advance to facilitate an effective but safe transition to patient care. Be sure to include patient caregivers in the planning of cross-training.

Data transparency is also vital to both employees and the community. Understanding healthcare data and metrics and how they apply personally will help employees and community members make health decisions based on facts.

COVID-19 MAGNIFIER: CRISIS SPURS CREATIVITY

The onset of the COVID-19 pandemic made clear the stark reality of supply chain challenges and the need to work with teams to care for patients. However, we have seen this crisis spur creativity. Here are a few examples:

- Healthcare employees developed masks out of a sterile wrap material as medical-grade masks became difficult to obtain. This prompted local businesses and citizens to start producing masks. In Denver, Colorado, the Hunter Douglas Company created masks from material used to make household blinds. Citizens formed sewing groups to make masks for the community.

- We saw the development of personal protective equipment (PPE) distribution stations to ensure the effective distribution of much-need supplies to hospital

(continued)

(continued from previous page)

employees and physicians. The stations provided appropriate equipment based on each employee's shift assignment. In addition, the stations reprocessed masks and returned them to assigned employees.

- Technology was vital to ensure that patients were able to communicate with family members. The use of iPads became a tool for caregivers to facilitate communication—often between a family and a dying patient. Additionally, iPads were used by physicians and other healthcare professionals to visit with patients without entering their rooms. This allowed for the conservation of PPE.

- New producers of hand sanitizer emerged. For example, local distilleries and hospital pharmacies began producing hand sanitizer to meet the demands of hospitals and communities.

- Baby monitors were purchased at local stores so that caregivers could listen for alarms on medication pumps and patient monitoring equipment because patients had to be isolated behind closed doors.

- Caregivers were concerned that hospitalized patients, who were already isolated, could not connect with nurses and physicians behind their extensive PPE. Photos and name tags were displayed on top of the PPE to let patients know who was caring for them.

- The Space for Grace virtual support group was one of many strategies implemented to help caregivers debrief and seek support during the crisis.

—*Lori Wightman*

STEP 10: CREATE A CULTURE OF INNOVATION AND CREATIVITY

If you don't establish a culture of innovation and creativity, you won't have it when you need it! Innovative approaches to empowering employee creativity during the pandemic came in handy for many healthcare systems.

Engage frontline employees in process improvement, workflow redesign, and the development of solutions. Make it safe for employees to solve problems (and sometimes fail) as they come up. You will need all levels of the organization responding in a crisis with empowerment, know-how, and creativity. *The Nurses' Guide to Innovation* is one excellent resource for creating an innovative mindset.[2]

*   *   *

These areas may seem like priorities that organizations would have had in place before the pandemic. However, the crisis has given us a new lens through which to examine our priorities. We may need to rethink our priorities to ensure that our organization emerges from the crisis.

NOTES

1. Koloroutis, M., and D. Abelson (eds.). 2017. *Advancing Relationship-Based Cultures.* Minneapolis, MN: Creative Health Care Management.

2. Clipper, B., M. Wang, P. Coyne, V. Baiera, R. Love, D. Nix, W. Nix, and B. Weirich. 2019. *The Nurses' Guide to Innovation: Accelerating the Journey.* Cupertino, CA: Super Star Press.

Creating a Culture Brand and Positioning Your Organization Competitively

THINK ABOUT THE vehicle you drive. What exactly led you to buy that particular make and model? Was your decision based on price, look, or performance? What drew you into the dealership? What was appealing about the dealer's advertising? Perhaps you heard good reviews from friends or family.

Just as you have the ability to choose the products you buy, highly skilled people have the ability to choose where they work. Today, employees can easily check online sources or their own personal networks to find out what it's like to work in your organization without even stepping through the front door. How you establish your culture brand and competitive positioning is critical to prospective employees as they decide whether to consider your organization for future employment. In this section, we will discuss how to shape organizational culture and which components you should pay attention to. When reading this chapter, don't get overwhelmed. An Organizational Culture Assessment Checklist is provided in appendix B.

CHAPTER 2

Shaping Culture Carefully

"BUT I TOLD them the policy committee is to be disbanded!" exclaimed a frustrated CEO. "I announced that I've decided policies will be approved by the area executive, and we will not be going through the committee anymore!" Instead of disbanding, the old policy committee went underground and insisted on meeting quietly behind the CEO's back. It became a "ghost" committee, influencing policies anyway, despite the words coming from the top.

That's culture speaking.

"Why isn't the needle moving on our customer engagement scores?" asked a CEO in a meeting with leaders. "I thought we agreed to this and other objectives as our top priorities. But the numbers are not changing in a positive direction, and our revenue is declining. What is going on?" The organization had set top-level objectives and engaged in many initiatives to accomplish those objectives. The CEO had called a leadership team meeting in the hope of learning why objectives were not being met. However, the room felt uncomfortable. Many of the leaders were nervously checking their smartphones, writing notes, or doodling. The CEO's questions were met with silence.

That's culture speaking.

Shock and disbelief overcame the leaders of a healthcare system on the West Coast when they learned of a patient who had died on a particular nurse's watch. A lot of money, people, and resources were thrown at the problem, such as training and setting performance expectations for proper quality protocols. Despite that effort, one night a nurse ignored the protocols that required staff to check on patients periodically through the night. She falsely stated in the file that the patient was alright, when in fact the paraplegic patient had slipped down between the bed mattress and rail, suffocated, and died. The nurse never checked on the patient, despite what she wrote in the file. When asked why she had documented an incorrect account of events, she replied, "That's how we do it here."

That's culture speaking.

WHEN CULTURE SPEAKS

Organizational culture will take a form of its own and speak for itself. A strong culture unites employees toward a common purpose that is aligned with the organization's mission, vision, and values—that is, with its "head and heart." A strong culture will attract talent like a magnet. What matters to employees in deciding where to work is what the culture is like. A strong organizational culture will guide leaders to make the right decisions based on values, especially during a crisis. However, the recent COVID-19 pandemic, economic upheaval, and civil unrest brought a day of reckoning for organizations worldwide. How well healthcare organizations are able to shift and adapt amid massive disruption will be felt by employees, patients, and communities for years to come.

THE CULTURE–LEADERSHIP DISCONNECT

Well-meaning leaders believe that all they have to do is utter words, set expectations, throw money and resources at a problem, or pressure HR to do something about it—and everything will magically fall in line. Tragically, culture is often seen as too nebulous, too hard, or too complex to wrap our minds around. A lot of people don't think about organizational culture until there is a problem. Or, sometimes people in leadership positions resist change, which sets the tone for the rest of the organization.

Success can be found when we think of organizational culture as a living thing. If organizational culture is left unmanaged or is only weakly managed, it can become dysfunctional or toxic. On the flip side, an intentionally nurtured organizational culture (or mini cultures) can make it possible to recruit and retain top talent, develop a solid brand, deliver a consistent customer experience, and, ultimately, increase revenue and ensure a viable future.

Which reality do you want?

WHAT IS ORGANIZATIONAL CULTURE?

To shape culture, it is necessary to understand what it is. *Organizational culture* refers to the shared norms, beliefs, and assumptions of individuals and groups within an organization. Organizational culture guides how individuals act and interact with others. When you hear people say things like "that's how we do it here"—*that* is culture. "We" = culture. The use of the word "I" is an indicator of personal responsibility. Organizations will only go as far as their culture will take or let them.

Think of it this way: Imagine you are a wild horse. You want to gallop and go far. Think of organizational culture as a tall fence that can't easily be jumped and goes deep into the ground. To go far, you have to go around the fence or change the dimensions of the fence.

HOW TO ASSESS CULTURE

Since organizational culture can derail organizational objectives, assessing your organizational culture is just as important as evaluating patient experience scores, financials, or quality outcomes. After all, organizational culture can be the reason why your other objectives are not being met. Ultimately, the workforce you are seeking is evaluating the organizational culture. Prospective employees can learn what it's like to work in your organization through websites such as Glassdoor.com or Indeed.com. They can also see what current employees are saying on social media.

Since culture functions as a living thing, it is very difficult to measure. What you can do is assess the strength of your organizational culture and the impact it has. In other words, you can look at symptoms of a weak culture or the positive impact of a strong culture.

The following questions can be used to assess your organizational culture:

- **What do you hear when you walk around your workplace?** Walk around and listen quietly to chatter in the halls. Eat lunch in the cafeteria and listen. Don't eavesdrop—listen to employees' tone of voice. Do employees seem relaxed? Or do they sound frustrated? Does their tone of voice align with your organization's mission and values? When walking around, observe elements of the workplace that influence culture, such as space, connectivity, communication, and tone. Do employees know you? Do they smile and offer polite communication?

- **What does your turnover look like?** Look objectively at your turnover rate. Resist the temptation to explain it away or water it down. Are your turnover numbers habitually high? Are they higher in one area than another? What do employees say in their exit interviews? On the flip side, are there areas where turnover is low and stays low?

- **What do job candidates think about when they see your organization's job posts?** It's a good idea to talk to your recruitment team rather than just pressuring them to hire more! The recruitment team typically has a good understanding of why prospects decline offers and what candidates are saying about your organization. They also have a good handle on what is happening in your organization and in each department. They can tell you whether a particular department has a toxic culture, making it more difficult to fill vacancies.

- **Does change stick?** Ask yourself and your team whether the change initiatives you have in place are actually working and staying in place. Just because a memo went out about a change, don't assume it is actually happening when you are not looking.

- **Is it a struggle to accomplish goals and objectives?** When it comes to achieving objectives, do you feel like you are herding cats? In other words, is everybody going their own way? Or do you have a culture in which everyone is pulling in the same direction, like a professional rowing team?

- **Are team members distant and silent, or are they fully engaged?** Organizational culture should create a place of safety to raise ideas about how to take on challenges and improve the patient experience. Distant or silent team members may indicate that the culture is toxic or that employees feel it's not safe to speak up. Does your culture encourage people to speak up and provide safety without fear of unfair judgment?

HOW LEADERS CAN SHAPE ORGANIZATIONAL CULTURE

True engagement connects the hearts and minds of employees to the mission and vision of an organization. Change happens at the emotional level. Culture can change one conversation at a time. It starts at the top and is executed in a department . . . every moment of every day. Leaders have a crucial role in shaping culture. The following sections discuss a few ways that leaders can begin to shape organizational culture.

Define the Ideal Culture and Gaps

Defining the ideal culture and gaps requires the senior leadership team to talk deliberately about what the organization needs to look like to be successful for years to come. It's better to be brave, discuss, and listen to those who know about the organizational culture—before culture speaks for itself. If you are a department leader, start with your division.

Don't get overwhelmed—start by answering two questions: What does the ideal culture look like, and what does it look like today? Go ahead, but be brave!

Employees Are Inspired by Purpose, not Posters

Having a great mission, vision, and values is a great start. Employees are inspired by purpose, not by motivational posters. Ask yourself whether employees can see themselves in your organization's mission, vision, and value statements. Do they understand that they can have an impact on and support the organization's mission, vision, and values? What about employees who are not actively interfacing with patients, families, or other customers? Connect the dots for everyone in the organization.

Leader Behavior Modeling

Culture starts from the top, with attitudes and tone modeled by leaders. An organization can be its own worst enemy when it enables toxic or weak leaders. Leaders who take a "do as I say, not as I do" approach will torpedo any hope of building a strong organizational culture.

It is critical to ensure that leaders are modeling the organization's values in every interaction, every day. Leaders are "on stage" inside and outside the organization. Behavioral expectations of leaders shouldn't be a secret. Leaders need to know how their behavior contributes to employees' desire and motivation to move the needle on results. Assuming that every leader understands or models ideal value behaviors, or has a complete skill set to be successful, is a mistake. How do your leaders treat employees and behave when you are not looking?

COVID-19 MAGNIFIER: RETAINING EMPLOYEES DURING FURLOUGH

We had never furloughed anyone before, but suddenly we were faced with letting 377 hard-to-recruit employees know we were "pausing" their employment. The local competition for talent was tough. We did a few things to keep them tied to us.

We paid the total cost for their health benefits for the 90-day furlough period. We communicated that our focus was to make sure they continued to have a paycheck for as long as possible. Their accrued paid time off remained in place. We created a temporary labor pool made up of employees whose hours had been cut so that we could redeploy them in roles we had never needed before (e.g., door screeners, COVID-19 test swabbers, other positions in the hospital) at their normal wage rate, regardless of the temp job.

The result: 98 percent of the furloughed staff came back.

—*Michele A. Talka, Chief Human Resources Officer,*
Central Maine Healthcare

Business Practices Alignment

Value statements are only as good as the paper you print them on if there isn't alignment within the organization. Think of the hundreds of communication touchpoints you have with employees: recruiting, onboarding, orientation, policies, training, meetings, committees, huddles, evaluations, corrective actions, coaching, emails, memos, newsletters, company picnics, celebrations, service awards, and so on. Do all of those business levers and messages align with the culture you wish to create? All of your business practices should support your ideal culture—otherwise, you are misaligned.

Measure and Monitor

Measuring culture as a stand-alone metric is hard to do. But there are ways to measure the *impact* of organizational culture. You can measure perceptions, attitudes, knowledge, and awareness, as well as resulting behaviors such as turnover and absenteeism. These measures are indicators of the health of your organizational culture.

Employee Engagement Surveys

Measuring organizational culture through employee engagement surveys requires not just chasing the score, but also putting action to what we learn. Key steps to utilizing surveys to promote a healthy organizational culture include the following:

- Get buy-in and input from senior leaders on the necessity of the employee engagement survey.
- Get a sense of where you stand with engagement and culture by analyzing employee and leader feedback and turnover trends.

- Set a goal or objective: What do you wish to accomplish by conducting an employee satisfaction survey? Examples include gaining insight into how to increase employee engagement and improve on organizational culture, increasing retention, and improving two-way communication between employees and managers.
- Share the details of the survey with employees. Transparency matters more than ever.
- Follow through on reasonable improvement areas and communicate what you've accomplished with employees.
- Celebrate wins! This step is just as important as making improvements. It tells employees what aspects of the culture are going well and what you wish to continue.

Exit Interviews

Exit interviews are another way to measure what's going on with your organizational culture. Ensure that the leaders who conduct the interviews ask consistent questions about the culture of the employee's work unit and the organization. The responses enable you to measure, monitor, and respond to matters as they are brought forward. Like the employee engagement survey, it is critical to take action on what you learn.

BLENDING CULTURES AFTER MERGERS AND ACQUISITIONS

Mergers and acquisitions (M&As) slowed down during 2020, no doubt as a result of the pandemic and economic downturn. However, year over year, there is no significant difference in M&A volume. This business strategy is still seen as a way to achieve economies of scale and leverage better care coordination, standardization, and population health management.

While there is debate as to whether M&As truly produce those desired benefits, our focus in this section is how to best manage M&As in a way that will attract and retain talented individuals rather than scare them off. If the newly formed entity can't retain or attract talent, the time, money, and resources spent on the transition will be wasted.

- Assess whether the two cultures are compatible. While a lot of thought goes into the financial and legal implications of M&As, cultural implications are often overlooked.
- Pick the best of both worlds. The goal of blending two cultures 100 percent is often met with failure. Each organization must set beliefs, values, and systems that make sense. Blending the best of both worlds, rather than bulldozing, is more likely to keep employees engaged. Retain the best practices, policies, and systems of each organization.
- Involve employees in the process when possible. Creating cross-functional teams that consist of employees from both organizations to work on logistics, process, and collaboration is a great path toward success.
- Communicate early and often with both organizations. Be as transparent as possible and be prepared to answer tough questions posed by employees.

The successful blending of cultures is tough work and happens over time. A commitment to nurturing cultures over time is a must.

LEADERSHIP ENGAGEMENT AND BOARD GOVERNANCE

Leadership Engagement

Leaders and organizational culture are forever linked—this is where the "rubber meets the road." Leaders influence organizational culture either consciously or unconsciously. The best leaders are engaged, fully aware, and own their part in shaping culture. They actively learn how to leverage organizational culture and sub-cultures to build on their business, and resist being confused or frustrated by it.

Board Governance

Since organizational culture can make or break a company's purpose and objectives, boards of directors must provide good governance oversight. Board members can take action in these key areas:

- Oversee how culture is defined and aligned with strategy.
- Establish leadership accountability for modeling culture, including the CEO, all executives, and mid-level and frontline leaders. From experience, it is best to establish an independent and confidential feedback system that doesn't rely solely on the internal CEO or a handful of executives. This will ensure honest checks and balances.
- Create a way to monitor culture growth through metrics or other methods.
- Ask questions about how strategy shifts such as financial or competitive changes will affect culture.
- Challenge the board's culture to ensure that it, too, is becoming stronger. Invite board members to walk the halls of the organization and speak with employees.

THE ART OF STORYTELLING

Relying on business statistics to persuade people to take action tends to fall flat. Deeply personal stories make messages powerful and bring hope. Stories let people decide for themselves what is important, leading to influence and inspiration. The best stories tug at the heart and stir an emotional response. A truly engaged employee is one who is emotionally connected to the mission and values of the organization.

When crafting stories effectively, leaders do the following:

- Think about the audience and what's in it for them.
- Have a call to action—think about how they want people to feel, think, or do.
- Know they are only as good as their last speech or communication.
- Make employees the heroes by encouraging them to tell their own stories.
- Focus on conveying honesty rather than reciting a branded script.

Shaping culture is for only those who are serious and sincere about raising the bar of performance. A strong and effective organizational culture doesn't happen by itself. Isn't it better to deliberately shape the culture and future, instead of letting the organizational culture take charge of you?

Retaining Employees—Because Keeping People Matters

"WE NEED TO HIRE MORE!" This phrase has been repeated by leaders more times than we can count. The recruitment team faces tremendous pressure. Without a focus on retaining employees, an organization becomes a revolving door through which people come and go.

This reality makes it hard to gain traction on organizational objectives relating to culture change, the patient experience, quality, safety, community care, and financial strength. Our patients and community, as well as employees and physicians, are counting on our ability to go beyond recruitment. Keeping people matters.

CHAPTER 3

Make It Matter—Engagement with a Difference

THE RECOGNITION OF frontline healthcare workers makes us proud—it is very much deserved. It can and has renewed the spirit of camaraderie and mutual support, which is what many employees long for in a workplace. Engaged employees feel supported and emotionally connected to what they do and to the organization's mission.

During a global health crisis, when the world is resting on the shoulders of healthcare workers, it's more critical than ever to engage and retain them. After all, it's not just about the patient satisfaction or employee engagement scores. The world depends on healthcare workers to save lives and support the sick and injured with the best care we can provide. That means the status quo has to go. We have entered into a new era in the workplace. We must make employee retention matter. Engagement efforts must make a significant and sincere difference going forward. The world is counting on it.

EMPLOYEE ENGAGEMENT VERSUS EMPLOYEE EXPERIENCE

It is common to use the words "engagement" and "experience" interchangeably, but this may cause confusion when setting objectives and strategies. To define what we are trying to achieve, it is important to understand the difference between these two concepts.

Employee engagement is the end goal—the "what." Employee experience is "how" we get an engaged workforce.

Think of experience this way: Remember the last time you went to a concert. A memorable concert experience goes beyond just buying a ticket. What makes a concert memorable is the ride to the venue with friends or family, standing in line, and enjoying refreshments. If it's a rock concert, it's not just about hearing the music but feeling the beat thunder from the speakers. It's being with people who like the same music and enjoying their company. It's the feeling of being lifted up by taking part in something fun and wonderful. Depending on your experience, you are engaged and can't wait to attend another concert.

Now imagine what a memorable experience would be like throughout the employee cycle in your organization—from recruitment through exit. What is the experience like for those working every day in the emergency department, finance, marketing, human resources, or clinical operations? What has the experience been like for your leaders and employees combating a global health crisis?

LET EXPERIENCE BE YOUR GUIDE: THE EMPLOYEE EXPERIENCE JOURNEY

"Experience journey" is a term borrowed from the marketing playbook that is used to map out and understand what it's like to be a patient. The same method can be used to map out the employee journey.

The journey spans recruitment to exit and every stage in between. It encompasses many moments, both good and bad. Not all moments along the journey are the same. It is best to map out employees' journeys through their eyes and involve them in the discovery process.

Mapping the journey can seem overwhelming. Breaking it up into key moments—what we like to call "touchpoints"—will make this discovery more manageable.

These touchpoints correspond to the stages of employment (a full employee journey map can be found in appendix C):

1. Recruitment and attraction
2. Hire and offer
3. Onboarding
4. Engagement
5. Performance
6. Development
7. Exit and separation

THE POWER OF FOCUS: IT'S IN THE SMALL THINGS

It might surprise you that what matters to employees goes beyond their paycheck. While getting paid fairly in exchange for work is an inherent expectation, it is the small elements of the employee experience that matter. Remembering to say thank you goes a long way in promoting employee engagement.

The visibility of leaders in rounding, providing regular meals and snacks, and offering groceries and frozen meals for employees to take home are important, especially during a worldwide crisis. Many organizations have deployed nonclinical staff to serve as helping hands for caregivers, performing nonclinical tasks such as running for supplies, answering phones, and responding to patient call lights.

One way to show that you care is to really *listen*—rounding, listening, and asking for feedback on barriers or opportunities, followed by action! It is hard to focus when circumstances are pulling leaders in many different directions. Keeping a focus on employee safety, especially during a pandemic, puts the words "we care about you" into action. Employees will remember these kinds of actions for a long time.

NAVIGATING BARRIERS: BURNOUT, CRISIS FATIGUE, GRIEF, AND DISENGAGEMENT

There are plenty of external barriers to employee engagement. But as leaders, we know about the internal barriers, too, such as dealing with burnout, disengagement, high anxiety, and crisis fatigue. This goes for employees and leaders alike. It is best to be clear on what exactly these concepts mean, so that we can create a plan to deal with them.

Burnout is a state of mental exhaustion, stress, and fatigue experienced by employees, leaders, and providers. Burnout is usually caused by unreasonable workload, stress, or strain over a long period of time.

While burnout among healthcare workers was already a priority before 2020, the introduction of a global pandemic and the long-term strains that came with it have made it even more important for leaders to address this barrier to engagement. Burnout alone is causing some people to choose not to enter the healthcare field at all and employees to leave it altogether.

Crisis fatigue has risen as a result of the pandemic and economic anxiety. People are weary of hearing one more piece of bad news.

Disengagement is the active withdrawal from a group or an activity. Burnout can lead individuals to detach themselves from the environment that is causing strain. Eventually, they may wish to leave, especially if they recognize that the environment is causing health problems or strain at home.

A Different Burnout Conversation

During the pandemic, we saw high levels of grief, moral distress, and acute stress. We have moved well beyond the normal conversation about burnout. Now, we must look past the typical recommendations for addressing burnout. Think about everything that the workforce has endured, not just professionally but personally—lockdowns, remote school, childcare closures, elections, wildfires and hurricanes, civil unrest and protests, and economic decline. Professionally, many employees have had to deal with the challenges of remote work, while frontline workers have been coping with an environment filled with uncertainty, fear, workforce shortages, exhaustion, and even physical harm (e.g., from wearing N95 masks for long hours). Despite these personal and professional challenges, employees in healthcare continued to deliver care. Frontline workers responded in heroic fashion.

Identifying and Measuring Burnout, Fatigue, and Anxiety

Burnout doesn't happen overnight. The warning signs can be subtle at first, so you'll need to pay close attention to your employees' well-being all the time. Red flags that require immediate actions include the following:

- Noticeable physical or emotional exhaustion
- Impatience or irritability
- Decreased productivity
- Frequent illness
- Increasing instances of unexcused absence, tardiness, or leave of absence

Burnout can be measured through employee engagement surveys, which capture employees' ability to activate and deactivate from work. These indicators show how well a workforce and its leaders can turn off their work minds. Studies show that healthcare workers easily activate because of their personal mission to care for others. It's turning off work that becomes a challenge for many.

Grief, Depression, and Acute Stress/Anxiety

We all experienced some level of loss during the pandemic. Loss comes in many forms:

- Loss of a friend, family member, or pet
- Loss of lifestyle through job loss or reduction of hours
- Loss of personal freedom as a result of lockdowns
- Loss of face-to-face connection and routine through remote work
- Loss of familiarity with the usual brands and supplies as a result of supply chain disruptions

Grief may manifest in many ways. The following are three common signs of grief:

1. Forgetfulness or distraction—uncharacteristically forgetting timelines, meetings, or follow-up details
2. Working less than normal—grief can weigh heavily on employees emotionally, causing disengagement from work or poor performance
3. Changes in relationships—suddenly isolating oneself from others or disengaging

This is the time for leaders to show they really care. But first, leaders need to understand the emotional impacts of a crisis; be able to identify the signs of grief, depression, and anxiety; know how to intervene; and know when professional help may be required. The following are some preventive or intervention steps:

- Give positive feedback on an ongoing basis
- Sincerely ask how your employees are doing and listen to their responses
- Treat everyone respectfully, even in stressful environments
- Rise above being just a "boss" to become a true leader
- Encourage the use of paid time off
- Help employees maintain a healthy work–life balance
  - Resist sending messages during off hours—it is too tempting to monitor emails and respond at all hours
  - Encourage remote employees to turn off work
- Step up mentoring and coaching efforts
- Provide support through Employee Assistance Programs, which may include therapist support and intervention

Build resilience back into your workforce. Resilience can be defined as the capacity to recover quickly, mental toughness, and the ability to spring back. When employees find meaning in their work, they are likely to remain deeply engaged for a long time. Employee assistance is not enough, however. Interventions must target employees' mind, body, and spirit; they should be offered in a variety of formats; and they should be applicable and useful to employees' professional and personal lives. Consider the diversity of the workforce (generational, ethnic, etc.) in designing interventions. Consider engaging ethics professionals and mission leaders (in faith-based healthcare) to combat moral distress among caregivers.

CHAPTER 4

Catch Them If You Can—
Retention Techniques

As HEALTHCARE LEADERS, it's easy to get caught up in the flurry of day-to-day activity—racing between back-to-back meetings, dealing with a multitude of crises, solving problems, looking for resources, and giving presentations to board members, leaders, or employees. The pace seems to quicken every day. It is easy to overlook the signs that a key employee is planning to exit the organization until it's too late.

An employee has given their two-week notice—now what? Do you have staff to pick up additional shifts, or will you need to get a traveler in place? Replacing a highly skilled individual will take longer than two weeks, causing a gap in productivity and putting additional strain on staff who are already struggling with burnout.

PROFIT BY PROACTIVE PREVENTION: QUANTIFYING TURNOVER COSTS

The standard turnover rate can be measured and analyzed in a variety of ways, such as per time period, per unit, per division, or per benchmark. While tracking the turnover rate is a good practice, it is even more desirable to apply meaning to that number. For example, what does turnover cost the organization?

Quantifying the true cost of turnover is difficult because often we are dealing with anecdotal information rather than hard numbers. Factors such as lost productivity, morale, and incidental expenses are hard to capture. But we know intuitively that these factors contribute to the high cost of turnover.

If you google the cost of employee turnover, you will get a generic number—for example, 1.5 times the employee's salary. But we need hard numbers to understand what we can reasonably manage. Don't settle for generic numbers.

Follow these steps to quantify and specify the cost of turnover in your organization:

1. List all the processes or factors related to voluntary employee turnover, such as the following:
   a. Recruitment (job ads, recruiter time, vendor assistance, advertising in magazines or at universities, job boards)
   b. Reduced productivity (of the employee who is leaving and those who will cover shifts)
   c. Overtime to cover shifts
   d. Interview time for managers, executives, and coworkers
   e. Background checks
   f. Drug screening
   g. Credential checks
   h. Training costs
   i. New employee learning curve (contributing to suboptimal productivity)
2. Identify all required data and formulas pointing to costs.
3. Plug the data into a model or spreadsheet.

Once you've collected these data and calculated the cost of turnover, you can see the true budgetary impact on your organization.

That knowledge gives you clear justification to invest in more effective ways to retain staff. The cost of turnover can be invested in programs and methods to retain them. To help you with this comparison, consider the following model:

Description	Cost
Cost of turnover per employee (in a specific job group, e.g., RN, LVN)	$X
Cost of additional paid day off per employee (in a specific job group)	$X
Cost of reduced health insurance premium per employee	$X
Cost of software to enable flexible scheduling per employee	$X

If you can reduce the cost of turnover by even a fraction, how much more could you invest in the programs that matter most to your employees? Wouldn't the investment in programs that engage and, ultimately, retain employees be worthwhile?

ALTERNATIVE TURNOVER MEASURES

The standard turnover rate is calculated as the number of employees who left the organization divided by the average number of employees during the month, multiplied by 100. But this measure only gives you so much information. When compared with benchmarks, it will tell you whether your organization is high, average, or low. But to get actionable information, consider taking a more creative approach to measuring turnover. Here are some alternative metrics to consider:

- **Employee net promoter score.** This measure is borrowed from marketing to measure promoters, passives, and detractors using this question: "How likely are you to recommend this company as a good place to work?" Compare this score with employee comments and other measures to get a fuller picture of employees' loyalty and their willingness to be ambassadors for your organization and brand. This metric becomes meaningful when leaders take ownership of and embrace their role in influencing employee engagement.

- **Retention rate by manager.** There is something to be said for highlighting and modeling leaders who have low turnover. Perhaps those leaders should stand as mentors.
- **High-performer versus low-performer turnover (also known as "regrettable turnover").** It's no secret that top performers are drawn to high-performance cultures. Measuring this factor will demonstrate what kind of culture you have.
- **Turnover by reason for leaving.** If turnover seems too overwhelming to tackle, considering tracking the reasons why people leave the organization, such as pay and benefits, safety, supervisor, coworkers, family relocation, and so on. Then pick one category to focus on. If pay and benefits are driving high turnover, focus on that. We are not saying you should give everyone a raise and call it a day. Rather, make small improvements, and then communicate and educate widely and frequently, to see whether perceptions shift.

CATCH THEM WHILE YOU CAN

What can we do before employees resign in the first place? In chapter 3, we discussed how retention is a part of navigating the healthcare workforce shortage. Highly engaged employees are less like to leave.

An experienced leadership team will focus on turnover as much as hiring new talent. We all know turnover is a great cost and drains organizational resources. Prevention of turnover is also a golden strategy for navigating the healthcare workforce shortage.

Stay Interviews

Stay interviews query existing staff to measure their satisfaction and likelihood of staying with your organization. These interviews can be formal or informal. Whichever approach you take, the interviews should be comfortable, mimicking a natural conversation. If you call employees to your office out of the blue, you will create anxiety for them.

Stay interview questions are formed in such a way that employees don't feel as if you are giving them the idea to quit. Rather, they get to the heart of what motivates your employees to come to work every day. Stay interview questions are also designed to detect what may cause employees to want to quit, before they write their resignation letter. Questions might include the following:

- What is the most exciting part of your job?
- If you could change something about your job, what would it be?
- What factors contribute to you doing your best work?
- What do you like best or least about the organization?
- What can I do to support you?

Rapid Response Team

We can understand what a rapid response team is as it relates to bedside care. A rapid response team is used in a healthcare setting to promote rapid assessment and treatment of patients whose clinical status is deteriorating but not in cardiac arrest.

We can apply the same concept to employee turnover. In this case, the rapid response team would identify triggers that alert a group of caring people who can help prevent a resignation in the making. Commitment and a dedicated team are required for this concept to be successful.

Triggers to watch for include, but are not limited to, the following:

- Excessive absences
- Coming in late or early
- Increased personal calls
- Longer breaks
- Reduction in productivity
- Loss of enthusiasm for the organization and its mission
- Delegation of work to others
- Lack of commitment to long-term projects
- Recent new degree or certification
- Lack of concern about a supervisor's perceptions
- Employment verification requests

HR technology has become more sophisticated and now allows machine learning. Machine learning can monitor trends over time, watch for signs of employee disengagement, and alert leadership to a potential turnover situation.

LEVERAGING TOTAL REWARDS

Whether compensation is the reason why employees leave is highly debated among scholars, managers, and human resources professionals. Employees often cite pay and benefits as one reason they leave. However, studies have shown that employees often have other reasons for leaving that they do not feel comfortable saying out loud. Pay is an easy answer. Because pay for many healthcare jobs is very competitive, employees can easily find another job with better pay and benefits.

One strategy for addressing turnover due to pay is to lead the market in pay and benefits. But that is not so simple, given the budget strain that it entails. There are other ways to leverage total rewards to encourage retention. Here are a few ways to explicitly link rewards to retention:

- Team-based incentives tied to lower turnover as a unit or department
- Paid time off based on seniority
- Spot bonuses to recognize hard work and work well done
- Customizable or personalized benefits that allow employees to shape their own solutions to meet their needs

TALENT MANAGEMENT

Talent management can help leaders focus on the high performers who are vital to retain. For example, leaders can offer assessment and development plans, coaching, and mentoring. Providing development opportunities is critical to retention.

We have found employee advisory councils to be a valuable retention strategy, as they help leaders hearing from the people they want to retain. You can create a council by selecting a diverse group of employees to provide regular feedback on the work environment, benefits, growth opportunities, engagement barriers, culture, market competitiveness, and so on.

Powering Value Through Organizational Effectiveness

ORGANIZATIONAL EFFECTIVENESS IS how efficiently and effectively a company achieves its objectives. An effective organization is well designed, runs smoothly, and produces desired results with minimal wasted resources, money, and time. The higher the organizational effectiveness, the higher the value produced for employees, patients, and the community.

CHAPTER 5

Alignment Is the Fuel for Performance

DRIVING ALONG THE FREEWAY, you realize that your arms are getting tired. You have been fighting the steering wheel for miles. The car is pulling to one side, causing it to drift. If you don't work to keep the steering wheel straight, you could wind up going completely off the road.

What's the problem?

Misalignment. Time to take the vehicle in for service.

When your vehicle is out of alignment, it is difficult to steer. The same is true of organizations: When your organization is out of alignment, it is difficult to attract and retain talent, much less to achieve your organizational objectives. Alignment is critical to narrowing the workforce shortage. Employees can see past a branding statement and know whether your organization is "walking the talk." They want to be part of an organization that has it together.

EXTERNAL AND INTERNAL ALIGNMENT

Alignment can be defined in two ways: external and internal. External alignment occurs when the organization is in the right place, at the right time, with the right set of capabilities to meet growing market demand. Internal alignment occurs when the organization is heading in the right direction with little internal friction stopping rapid and effective execution. In other words, everyone is steering in the same direction.

When there is internal alignment, the organization can be agile and responsive to maneuver around potholes. It does not necessarily mean that everyone is in agreement or on the same page. Teams should be composed of people with complementary skill sets and diverse backgrounds and opinions. The key is having a culture of respect, integrity, and effective communication. All viewpoints are heard, considered, and then used to build an organizational vision or strategy. (For a detailed Organizational Alignment Assessment Checklist, see appendix D.)

SIGNS OF MISALIGNMENT

If you wondering why your organization is having difficulty moving the needle on your objectives, you may want to check your alignment.

Look for these signs of misalignment:

- Executives think in terms of the organizational chart (boxes and lines) and not system alignment.
- Leaders do not have the same focus or the same agenda.
- Organizational design is left to chance and to the inexperienced.
- Activities are mistaken for results or progress—much like tactics are mistaken for strategy.
- Complexity rules the day—confusion and disputes abound because of a lack of clarity on roles and responsibilities.
- There are too many meetings and not enough time to execute strategy.
- Communication and strategy development occur in silos— everyone is serving their own interests or those of their team.

- Decision-making takes too long.
- A lack of vision leads teams down diverse, winding roads—it is difficult to perform as a well-oiled machine when all the parts are moving in different directions.
- Turnover is high at all levels of the organization.
- Recruitment is difficult because the word is out—the organization is not aligned.

HOW TO CORRECT MISALIGNMENT

Align Organizational Direction

It's easy for leaders and departments to get caught up in their own agendas, which sometimes may conflict with one another. Misalignment can occur overtly or through scope creep. But it is important to occasionally "level set" everyone's understanding of the organization's overall direction.

How do we level set? Provide clear, regular, effective communication. Tie all strategy and organizational decisions and direction to the mission, vision, and values. Do leaders and employees match up in their focus? Make sure events, meetings, and projects are in alignment with the organization's needs and overall direction. Evaluate and stop work that does not contribute in some way to the mission, vision, and values. Goals should be cascaded to every individual in the organization and modeled by leaders (i.e., walk the talk). Expectations and goals must be understood by everyone.

Align Organizational Structure

Understanding who is responsible for what, which skills are necessary and which are lacking, and which processes need to be integrated is as important to alignment as common goal setting. In addition, silos are just as much an organizational structure problem as a leader mindset problem. We have seen organizations that believe they are being creative or "strategic" when in fact they have only built silos upon silos, layers upon layers, with no real connections in between.

Dump the existing organizational chart. List key deliverables that the organization must accomplish, and then right next to those deliverables, which leaders and departments are directly responsible for them. In cases in which departments and leaders are indirectly linked to all deliverables, those might be areas that should report to an overarching leader who is responsible for multiple deliverables.

Align Management Execution

Establish measures and short- and mid-range objectives and then ensure the leadership team is executing toward them. This is where we remove roadblocks or provide resources to get the job done. It is also important to monitor and communicate progress or lack of progress toward objectives.

Develop leaders to ensure they have the skill set necessary to effectively communicate and execute organizational strategy, tactics, and goals.

Align Budgets and Rewards

Not having a proper budget can prevent any leader from accomplishing objectives—particularly in organizations in which overspending is prohibited. Further, compensation and incentives are a powerful and often misunderstood resource that can align and propel the organization toward its objectives.

Leaders must be good stewards of resources. They must have the ability to move funding to and from projects. Ensure well-designed project plans and inspire your workforce to accomplish anything.

Align Communication

Inspire others by cascading the vision, purpose, and direction to all levels of the organization. If those in leadership positions are not communicating with their employees, find out why and influence a better outcome. Follow up and follow through on good internal communication practices.

Organizational misalignment is real and more common than leaders realize. It could be the one thing that is blocking your ability to attract and retain talent and achieve overall success. The good news is that alignment can be accomplished. Once you have the direction, tools, and tactics you need to unify your team, clarify accountability, and encourage cross-functional collaboration, the result will be an effective organization that provides exceptional value to customers and employees.

CHAPTER 6

Strategic Collective Bargaining

Healthcare organizations that have collective bargaining agreements with employee unions no doubt feel as if they are being squeezed. Even before the pandemic, cost-cutting measures and changes to benefit or compensation plans provoked the threat of a strike. The situation is even tighter during the pandemic. From the beginning of the pandemic, labor unions were vocal in their concerns about hospitals' ability to protect staff and patients. Since then, the divide between labor and organizational leadership has become wider and deeper.

On the labor side, we hear about:

- Inadequate staffing levels
- Lack of personal protective equipment (PPE)
- Low pay
- Retaliation for raising safety concerns
- Perceptions of uncaring administrators

Meanwhile, on the management side we hear:

- Lack of funds for raises
- Nationwide staff shortages
- Nationwide PPE shortages

- Pushback against charges of retaliation
- We care!

The pandemic is just one challenge facing the healthcare industry. Employers will surely face additional pressures in the future. We anticipate the expansion of employment laws and regulations, as well as a push to expand the provisions of the National Labor Relations Act and to raise the minimum wage. Only time will tell which regulatory changes will become law. Savvy employers will keep an eye on these developments and think through tactics to navigate change successfully.

STRATEGIZING COLLECTIVE BARGAINING

Taking a strategic approach to collective bargaining means starting early and planning proactively. It means starting well before both parties show up at the bargaining table.

Brainstorm—Set Limiting Beliefs Aside

A good practice before beginning the collective bargaining process is for the leadership team to have a deliberate discussion about what must be accomplished when contracts come up for bargaining. At this stage, don't let the fear of a strike, cynicism, or contentious history hold back the discussion. Brainstorm to get all ideas—old ones and fresh ones—out in the open.

Understand the Impact

Once you've done some brainstorming, determine the benefit and the expense of those ideas. Will they cost more or save money? If an idea costs more, will it improve the patient experience? How will the proposed changes impact quality of care, throughput, and employee retention? Dig deep and determine the impact of every option.

Set Priorities

Now that you understand the impact of each bargaining item, which should rise to the top of your priority list? What items are "must haves" for your organization to move forward in the years to come? Which ideas can wait?

Consider the Other Side

What does the other side want? More money? More benefits? Greater guarantees of safety? You can learn what employees want by listening to frontline and floor supervisors, paying attention to the petitions and complaints you receive, and even by reading union flyers. From a budgetary perspective, it may be painful to hear, given the financial constraints that healthcare organizations face. But this information becomes part of your strategic arsenal.

ZERO-SUM GAME

"It's a zero-sum game," the CFO responded every time we approached him during a bargaining period. "The money has to come from somewhere." Of course, getting what we wanted in the next contract meant agreeing to spending more money the other side wanted. This contract came on the heels of the Great Recession of 2008, and we could certainly understand the CFO's frustration.

(continued)

(continued from previous page)

My HR team and I went back to the drawing board and began to discuss where we could find the money to finance the contract proposals.

A team member noted that one of our pay practice policies had few controls in place, and as a result, the health system was losing millions of dollars. Analysis showed us that adding controls to this policy would save $4.6 million per year. We were on to something, and dug into other pay practices. Ultimately, we were able to finance the three-year union contract and achieve a zero-sum result.

—*Tresha Moreland*

MAP OUT YOUR BARGAINING STRATEGY

Once you have a handle on what the union wants, initiate a trade strategy. "We will give you this if you give us that." If your desired goal will save money, perhaps you can finance the union's requests and more.

This is also a prime time to revisit who should attend the bargaining session. Do you have a finance analyst who can quickly model proposal costs? What about employees who have a clear understanding of how staffing works? Make sure you have all the right people at the bargaining table.

COLLECTIVE BARGAINING ACCOUNTING

There is a strategic benefit to having a finance professional at the bargaining table or in a room nearby. Being able to quickly quantify not just proposals made by the union, but also ideas from your health system leadership, is a creative strategy.

Sometimes ideas will occur spontaneously during collective bargaining. Those ideas may help bring the collective bargaining to a successful conclusion. Being able to rapidly quantify ideas and seek approval from health system leaders is a good strategy.

Savvy finance professionals can develop sophisticated modeling tools that enable them to quickly run the numbers. These models typically build in the number of employees in a particular unit, wages, the cost of benefits, as well as references to pay practice policy costs.

WHAT LIES AHEAD

We knew what to expect under the Donald Trump administration. However, expectations going forward are still unclear. All employers, whether union or not, should pay attention!

In the future, it will be essential for nonunion departments and organizations to focus on developing authentic relationships with their workforces. Proactively conducting vulnerability assessments and establishing "go-to" plans in the event of organizing activity is smart.

For union employers, there is no perfect solution to the collective bargaining process. You may face many days of frustration ahead. It is our hope that strategic thinking in the bargaining process will help move the needle on critical initiatives.

Leveraging Recruitment in a Disrupted World

HEALTHCARE IS ONE of the largest employers in the United States, accounting for more than 16 million jobs, or nearly 11 percent of all jobs in the economy. Employment in healthcare occupations is projected to grow 15 percent from 2019 to 2029, adding about 2.4 million jobs.[1] Filling existing vacancies and staffing new jobs in light of the current workforce shortage puts a great deal of strain on recruitment efforts.

Other disruptive forces affect recruitment efforts as well: increasing competition for the same talent pool, skill gaps, generational shifts in the population, and the introduction of new technologies and social media platforms. We also must cope with the ways in which the COVID-19 pandemic has destabilized the workforce by creating fear, anxiety, and stress at the highest levels. We will explore shifting forces and how to leverage them in chapter 9.

We understand that investing time and money in recruitment is a tough balancing act for most healthcare organizations. The need to manage unforgiving financial constraints and juggle multiple priorities, projects, and shifting directions has created unrelenting pressures on healthcare leadership. However, there is no disputing that recruitment is a key lever that must be pulled to navigate the workforce shortage. As healthcare leaders, if we don't think differently about how we recruit talent, our organizations may be left behind.

In this section, we examine leveraging recruitment more effectively by considering both internal strategies and external strategies. Both play critical parts in the bigger picture of attracting hard-to-recruit talent. A Recruitment Effectiveness Assessment Checklist, found in appendix E, can be used alongside these two chapters.

NOTE

1. US Bureau of Labor Statistics. 2020. "Healthcare Occupations." *Occupational Outlook Handbook*. Updated September 1. www.bls.gov/ooh/healthcare/home.htm.

CHAPTER 7

Internal Recruitment Strategies

HEALTHCARE ORGANIZATIONS HAVE many internal strategies and tactics available to navigate the challenges of the workforce shortage. However, many of these internal resources may be overlooked because leaders adhere to status quo approaches to recruitment.

Leaders who challenge themselves to think differently can successfully navigate the workforce shortage not just today, but in the long term. Doing so requires leaders to move outside their comfort zones and consider new approaches that may have an impact on recruitment. Sometimes just trying something new leads to extraordinary results.

To move beyond the status quo, examine the key internal areas discussed in this chapter to develop new strategies. Recruitment is not just the purview of HR. Partnership between HR and hiring leaders is vital. Leaders take ownership of recruitment in their areas of influence. They proactively monitor their staffing levels and reach out to experts in HR to brainstorm different ways to recruit and retain talent. Leaders may utilize their own social networks to post jobs and develop relationships with prospective employees.

KNOW YOUR NUMBERS

Demographic, market, and competitive pressures change frequently and unexpectedly. However, our long-standing assumptions may not. For example, a hiring manager may assume that a strong source for recruitment is a local university, and the manager may be satisfied with that source. But if another organization starts recruiting from the same source, the competition could cause a disruption in the unit's ability to staff. Worse, that competitor may implement a sign-on bonus that threatens to deplete the unit of its critical human resources. To combat these kinds of outdated assumptions, organizations need to have a deep understanding of their numbers and how they can be influenced. This section reviews several key numbers to know well: recruitment sourcing statistics, seasonal fluctuations in hiring, the application drop-off rate, and the offer acceptance rate.

Recruitment Sourcing Statistics

Sourcing is a must-have strategy for recruitment. Sourcing is the way viable candidates are identified to fill a vacant position. Organizations can draw on a number of sourcing channels, such as job boards, social media, the organization's website, employee referrals, job fairs, universities, and so on. Measuring the effectiveness of each source is not only smart but also cost-effective. If your organization is pouring money into a recruitment source that does not yield qualified hires, it is best to review that source and apply those funds elsewhere.

If you work for an organization that is tight on funds, we recommend investing in the top five or so sources that yield hiring results. Then apply the remaining funds in areas that you have not yet tried, such as specialty associations or recruitment fairs, to see whether they will produce new hires. Not only will you be utilizing existing funds for better use, but you also will be exploring new avenues in the event that an existing source dries up. This evaluation effort should be ongoing. Conducting a periodic review of your recruitment sources' effectiveness is a smart idea. It really doesn't matter what kind of system you use to track the effectiveness of your sourcing channels—just track it.

Sourcing is critical to recruitment, so it's a good idea to periodically brainstorm scenarios that could positively or negatively impact your source. For example, if a recruitment source dries up, what then? What sources should you optimize? Which sources are not yielding qualified hires? What other sources should you try?

Seasonal Fluctuations

Qualified candidates are constantly becoming available for new job opportunities, but the timing is often random. For example, the spouse of a qualified candidate is being transferred by the military and is moving to your area. A candidate has family obligations and will be relocating. A candidate wants to return to the place he grew up and will be moving to your area. The reasons are countless. But there also may be seasonal time frames when candidates are more open to exploring new opportunities than others.

Perhaps qualified candidates are tired of the cold weather and want to move to a warmer climate. Or new graduates are completing their required academic work and will be open to new opportunities in the spring. Maybe your organization is close to a tourist attraction that draws people during certain seasonal time frames.

We recommend that you study the reasons why people move to your state and city. Understand those trends and their seasonal fluctuations. From there, you can refresh your recruitment strategies to capitalize on those trends.

Application Drop-Off Rate

The candidate experience should be top of mind for healthcare leaders. The ideal candidate experience requires the application process to be simple. Think about it—most of the qualified candidates we need are already working. The only time they may have to look at your job post is during a 30-minute lunch break. The best way to get in front of candidates today is through their mobile phones.

Generationally speaking, baby boomers, Generation Xers, and some millennials may use the desktop version of your career website, but you won't see Generation Z there. While it is fun to examine generational differences, the truth is that all generations value quality of life and convenience over the aggravation of filling out an application form. If the application process is too hard to manage on a mobile device, you likely will lose candidates to competing organizations that have figured out mobile recruitment strategies.

If your applicant tracking system was built during the Stone Age, your application drop-off rate is probably on the rise. Losing even five qualified nurses during the application process can impact a unit's staffing and ability to reduce the high cost of contract labor.

We recommend that you review your application process. You can do so in a few ways. For instance, check out online sources such as Glassdoor.com that ask candidates to review organizations' hiring processes. Another way is to go through the application process yourself: Pretend to apply for a job and have your internal teams take you through the process step by step as if you were a real candidate.

When was the last time you applied for a job through your organization's standard hiring process? Now is a good time to revisit that process and go through the candidate experience journey yourself.

Offer Acceptance Rate

The offer acceptance rate measures the percentage of candidates who accept your job offers. This measure helps determine the overall success of your employment brand and recruitment efforts.

If the majority of candidates are accepting your job offers, your recruitment process is working well. However, if the acceptance rate is dropping, something is wrong, and the process is worth examining.

Candidates may not be turned off by the compensation part of the offer. The process could be too slow, causing candidates to lose interest and move onto another organization. Or perhaps your organization has a poor reputation, and that is causing candidates to change their minds. We recommend tracking the offer acceptance rate monthly or quarterly to keep tabs on the effectiveness of your recruitment efforts.

TEAM POWER

Boosting recruitment power is the single most important strategy in a world of workforce shortages. Whether recruitment efforts are internal, external, or a hybrid of both, team members must be aligned and coordinated with each other. They must perform like a rowing crew. The last thing you want is your recruitment team members competing for the same candidate. Leaders should consider which recruitment model is best for their organization.

A centralized recruitment model is an optimized delivery model that employs a centralized support service. Specifically, this model includes dedicated recruitment partners who work on the hiring manager relationship, understand the hiring manager's and departmental needs, manage the candidate experience, and source candidates. These individuals are assigned to a department, geographic area, or business unit.

In this model, a centralized sourcing team can manage all inbound, active candidate flow, develop direct sourcing strategies, manage internal candidates, and manage social media strategies. Best practice support models typically include recruitment coordinators, technology support, college and community outreach, diversity initiatives, metrics tracking, education, and vendor management.

SMALL OR RURAL ORGANIZATIONS

While the model just described may fit midsize to large healthcare systems, small or rural healthcare organizations may not have the resources to staff a large recruitment team. These organization may consider redesigning jobs to enable people in other roles or locations to recruit talent.

Increasing sourcing time is a key strategy that is always worth the effort. You may not need to have a recruitment team within the HR department that can make calls and track down potential candidates.

ONBOARDING PROGRAM

A rural health system in the Midwest developed an onboarding program for new hires. The organization was losing qualified candidates to competing organizations because of the length of the hiring process. In addition, turnover of nurses in the first year exceeded 30 percent.

The onboarding program started with a candidate's initial contact with the organization (generally through a recruiter) and continued through the employee's first year of employment. The program began as a nursing initiative aimed at better managing candidates and retaining new nurses through their first year. The initiative was led jointly by a nurse leader and an HR leader. They engaged a multidisciplinary team that included frontline employees to design the onboarding program.

Performance improvement tools were used to map out the current process for recruiting and onboarding new nurses. Significant gaps were identified in the process. Then, the team did its research, looking at

(continued)

(continued from previous page)

literature reviews, interviews with leaders in high-performing organizations, and surveys and interviews of recent hires, students, and current job seekers. Once the research was complete, the team designed a best-practice onboarding process. The new process had clear tasks, timelines, assigned accountabilities, and metrics to measure the success of each phase of the program. The program not only generated the needed outcomes, but also created an effective, strong relationship between nurse leaders and HR colleagues. The program eventually was used to onboard all employees. The program implemented several new onboarding strategies:

- Hiring managers were expected to respond to candidates within 24 hours. While the team agreed that this was a best practice, it was challenging to operationalize. Hiring managers created an "on-call" schedule to manage candidates. Each evening, the on-call manager would review the candidates sourced during the day and call each candidate. Interview appointments were made using a shared calendar in which managers highlighted the times they were available to conduct interviews.

- HR and nurse leaders developed an onboarding packet that was sent to new hires at least one week before their start date. The packet included a handwritten welcome note from the hiring manager, information about their assigned preceptor (including a photo), an overview of their new work unit, and a tentative schedule for their first month.

(continued)

(continued from previous page)

- The program included a meet-and-greet with the nurse executive, lunch with their new manager, and routine meetings with their manager for the first year—biweekly to start, and then decreasing in frequency over time. A preceptor was assigned to learn the role (skill acquisition), and a mentor was assigned to ease the transition into the organization and unit culture.

—*Tresha Moreland and Lori Wightman*

TOGETHERNESS

Leveraging cross-functional collaboration is a powerful internal strategy. Great things can happen when organizations harness the power of collaboration between HR and operational teams to implement recruitment initiatives. When cross-functional teams work together, they can generate fresh ideas, share key information, save time, and avoid the risk of hiring the wrong candidates. Teams that share information—especially for the first time—may have aha! moments when they realize how much more productive they can be when they are working together.

This may seem elementary, and it should already be happening in our organizations. However, it is not unusual to have silos at work. If you aren't watching closely, those silos can creep into the culture before you are fully aware of their full impact on the organization. Organizational silos come in several different types. For example, people in departmental silos may have minimal interactions with those outside their department.

Another type of silo is an information silo. People may talk or even meet regularly, but their information systems do not interconnect. This type of silo makes key data invisible to other teams. For example, HR may have access to information about the hiring pipeline, such as how many nurses have accepted an offer, but nursing managers may not necessarily have access to that information. As a result, nursing managers may make staffing decisions to bring on expensive contract labor without realizing that nurses have been hired and are making their way through the onboarding and training processes. Or, the nursing managers may have sole access to staffing information. If HR managers do not have access to this information, they may be unaware of staffing needs and the imperative to begin recruitment activities.

Take time to observe your teams. Consider whether they are connecting well and have the information they need to be effective. If silos exist, consider the following ways to create cross-functional work groups:

- Get executive buy-in and support for a collaborative approach and the time and resources to support it.
- Create a shared vision that makes clear that we are better together.
- Set expectations early and often.
- Ensure that accountability for actions is clearly defined.
- Make it safe to share new ideas.
- Encourage teams to build relationships with each other.
- Remove information silos and roadblocks.
- Centralize communication and data access.
- Make it easy to form cross-functional teams and collaborations.
- Experiment with new technologies and new ways to pull teams together, both in person and electronically.
- Recognize and celebrate team wins, milestones, and goal attainment.

REALIGNMENT: JOBS, SKILLS, PRACTICE FLOW, AND TEAM MODELS

Reskilling and Redeployment

A key strategy for navigating a workforce shortage lies in our existing talent pools. The practice of utilizing and redeploying existing resources is on the rise. In healthcare, this trend is even more important because of changing skill needs as well as the shrinking workforce pool. Reskilling and redeployment can and should be leveraged for organizational success.

The terms *upskilling* and *reskilling* are often used interchangeably. Upskilling is the process of adding new skills so that an employee can successfully perform a different type of job. For example, a licensed practical nurse may return to school and earn a registered nurse license to be able to do a different job. Reskilling involves replacing old skills with new ones so that an employee can continue to perform the same job. For example, an employee in the information technology department may learn additional skills to train others to use a new electronic health record system while in the same job.

The benefits of reskilling or upskilling strategies are more far-reaching than just filling a staffing gap. They can also be instrumental in retaining employees, maintaining institutional knowledge, and enhancing the employer's brand as a great place to work. Redeployment can meet an employee's need for developmental opportunities and upward or lateral career advancement.

The following are some ideas to approach reskilling and redeployment:

- **Develop visual and interactive career paths.** Make it easy for employees to learn about career options within the organization and how to obtain those roles. Employees don't have time to find and read a ten-page job description to understand how to become a registered nurse.

- **Create personalized development plans.** Each employee has different personal and professional experience and skills. A personalized plan makes it real for employees. Develop a plan that includes clear training goals and milestones, and track employees' progress.
- **Use relatable case studies.** Testimonials from fellow employees are powerful tools for recruiting people into a program. Once the program is underway, consider using video testimonials from those who have successfully completed the program. Provide webinars and team workshops to encourage employees to learn more.
- **Offer mentoring.** Mentoring is popular because learning from another employee enhances the value of the experience. Mentors can help employees gain new skills that are not easily learned from reading a book.

Physician Practice Flow and Team-Based Care

Utilization of advanced practice providers such as physician assistants and nurse practitioners is becoming a necessity as workforce shortages become more severe. According to the US Bureau of Labor Statistics, employment of physician assistants is projected to grow 31 percent by 2029—much faster than the average for all occupations.[1]

Surgical practices have found that utilizing advanced practice providers to conduct rounds and postoperative visits provides more time for surgeons to be in the operating room. In medical practices, hiring advanced practice providers to handle clinic appointments can increase clinic capacity, thereby improving access to care and patient satisfaction.

Team-based care models will continue to evolve and grow. The team-based approach involves a combination of physicians, nurses, physician assistants, pharmacists, social workers, case managers, and other healthcare professionals. Because each healthcare system is unique, each team should be crafted based on population needs and relevant state laws.

Reviewing practice flows and augmenting those flows with advanced practice providers or physician assistants can help address workforce shortages as well as address burnout, create efficiencies, and improve engagement, quality, safety, and the patient experience.

Redefining Retirement

Another approach to navigating workforce shortages is to redefine retirement. After all, retirement is another train waiting to run us over if don't reroute the tracks, as discussed in the book's introduction. Holding onto employees who are thinking about retirement and enticing those who have retired back to the workplace is a smart approach.

Some healthcare organizations are redesigning the role of the registered nurse. Some nurses want to continue working, but on their own schedules. Flexibility is paramount in recruiting retired professionals to rejoin the workforce. Leveraging existing resources such as float pools, weekend work programs, and flexible schedules to define a program that will appeal to this demographic can help fill vacant shifts and hours despite workforce shortages.

RETAINING RETIRING NURSES

A community hospital in the Midwest was losing about half its operating room nurses to retirement over a two-year period. While the recruitment of experienced nurses is always a challenge, finding experienced operating room nurses is especially difficult: At the beginning of 2020,

(continued)

(continued from previous page)
more than 1,500 positions were posted on the website of the Association of periOperative Registered Nurses, a national professional organization. Senior nurses often are put off by long work hours, on-call demands, and inflexible scheduling. In response, this hospital created positions in which senior nurses could work four-hour shifts, schedule hours in advance, and avoid weekly shift requirements. These senior nurses provided relief during break and lunches, covered for employees who had personal appointments, conducted educational programming, and served as mentors.

The program was a huge success. Not only did the hospital retain more senior nurses for a longer period of time, but the program also improved overall retention and employee satisfaction, and it provided an avenue to develop skilled nurses for the future. The program was later introduced in other departments of the hospital.

—*Tresha Moreland and Lori Wightman*

OVER-HIRE STRATEGY

Another approach to recruitment is to apply an *over-hire* strategy, in which an organization projects the number of vacancies over a period of time and then hires and orients more new staff than originally projected to meet the anticipated vacancies. This strategy is useful in light of the long lag time between a resignation and the time a position is filled—plus the time it takes for a position to go through the approval process and for employees to be oriented and trained, increasing the organizational burden. Staff turnover may increase as well as employees experience heavier workloads as a result of vacancies. Organizations often feel they have no choice but to post the job and call in expensive contract labor to fill the gap.

Having a ready-made pipeline of workers who can step in at a moment's notice can increase efficiency in filling job openings and reduce turnover. But executives who are mindful of the financial pitfalls of "FTE creep" may be concerned about using an over-hire strategy. Having a good tracking process in place is crucial to ensure a balance between filling vacancies quickly and maintaining fiscal responsibility. If the strategy fills vacancies quicker and reduces contract labor, the strategy may be worth the effort.

We have placed this strategy in the internal recruitment section because the choice to use this strategy must come from the organization's leadership. This strategy may also overlap with those presented in chapters on retention, as lightening workloads and alleviating burnout for employees is another way to reduce turnover.

Strong recruitment starts with internal approaches that will attract candidates. Developing better, faster ways to tap into internal resources will make external recruitment efforts all the more effective. These internal strategies can be just the thing to help you navigate the workforce shortage.

NOTE

1. US Bureau of Labor Statistics. 2020. "Physician Assistants." *Occupational Outlook Handbook*. Updated September 1. www.bls.gov/ooh/healthcare/physician-assistants. htm#tab-6.

CHAPTER 8

External Recruitment Strategies

THERE IS NO magic bullet when it comes to quickly filling vacancies for highly skilled positions. Now that the bad news is out of the way, there is good news—but it's going to take some work, not just in your HR department but in the entire organization.

Successful recruitment involves developing relationships over time. Today, prospective employees are not just looking for a paycheck. The people you wish to recruit want to understand what kind of experience they will have in your work environment. The ideal goal for all organizations is for their workforce to reflect the diversity of the community it serves.

Prospective employees want to connect, belong, and experience. Job candidates want to understand what it's like in your work environment. The professionals you want to attract are looking at your leadership, organizational culture, and brand—what people are saying about you online. Your reputation will make or break your ability to recruit top talent. As we discussed at length in chapter 2, addressing organizational reputation goes beyond branding scripts or snazzy job ads.

Successful recruitment requires patience, persistence, creativity, and collaboration. Don't be afraid to test different methods. If those methods don't work today, consider whether they might work tomorrow under different circumstances. This chapter explores a variety of external recruitment methods.

START YOUNG

A long-term strategy to build your pipeline is to start young. It's not just other health systems that you are competing against, but also other career paths. Find your way into high schools to educate students about the many opportunities that are available in healthcare. You can get students excited and build loyalty toward your organization by teaching a class or sponsoring school events. For example, you could develop a program that targets high school students interested in becoming medical assistants as an entry point into the healthcare industry.

TAP INTO UNIQUE AND DIVERSE TALENT POOLS

It's time to kick status quo recruitment approaches to the curb and rethink how and where we look for talent. By status quo, we mean the standard "post and pray" method and other ways of recruiting "because we've always done it this way." In this era of workforce shortages, even the most beautiful ads may still yield crickets in the application system today.

The US population continues to become more diverse. Demographic shifts span race, national origin, and age. While the demographics of our patients and residents may change, reports indicate that workforce diversity efforts are not keeping up.

Following the death of George Floyd, concerns about diversity rose above pandemic worries. Many organizations issued PR statements and developed shiny new taglines meant to showcase their commitment to diversity. However, skilled talent can see beyond PR statements. Prospective employees look at the culture of each organization as they consider their next employment opportunity.

If there is anything to learn here, it is this rule of thumb: The greater the diversity commitment throughout the organization, starting with leadership, the greater the ability to attract and retain diverse talent. After all, a competitive advantage for any organization is one that embraces different and diverse opinions. Commitment is not a one-and-done item on a checklist. It requires a daily pledge by leadership to walk the talk. Make it safe to be different and to express distinct opinions. Otherwise, you lose the ability to attract and retain a diverse workforce.

If you haven't done so already, now is the time to step back and consider alternative recruitment sources to locate willing and able people. Have you considered different sources of skilled talent? Consider these groups who may be underrepresented in your workforce:

- People over age 50
- Veterans
- Individuals with disabilities
- Seasonal or "gig" workers
- People with a criminal justice history
- International candidates

Once you find different sources of talent, you will need to go beyond the "post and pray" method and seek out job boards that specialize in different sources of talent. Think of ways to develop relationships with a variety of groups of prospective employees. Posting on a job board and advertising the list of benefits you offer is not enough. You must be able to consistently demonstrate a good work environment, day in and day out, through your leadership, culture, and employees. Create avenues for prospective candidates to see what it's like to work in your environment and live in your location.

MAXIMIZE TECHNOLOGY AND SOCIAL MEDIA

Given tight budgets, investing in enterprise resource planning or HR information systems is a tough financial pill to swallow for many organizations. But studies indicate that the candidate experience is a key element of developing a good reputation and attracting talent.

As executives, we may land a job through the help of executive recruiters. But think of the recruitment experience from the employee's perspective. Here is a likely scenario in an organization that hasn't invested in HR technology: While on a break, a prospective candidate spots your job posting online. She whips out her smartphone and clicks the "Apply on Company Site" button. The link takes the candidate to a site where she needs to register and upload her résumé. The site tells her that her user ID already exists and asks her to log in. Thinking she must have forgotten that she had applied for a job with this company before, the candidate tries to log in. But what was the password? She hits "Forgot Password," only to receive an error message. Time's up—the candidate's 30-minute break is over, and she doesn't have time to figure out her password.

Now consider the same scenario for a competitor organization who has invested in HR technology. The next day, the same candidate spots another job posting from a competing organization. She whips out her smart phone to apply. She clicks on the link that says "Easy Apply." It takes the candidate to a page that asks if she wants to send a social media profile to the employer. She clicks "yes," and the profile is sent. The candidate receives an email or text message inviting her for an interview. She is hired.

IT TAKES A VILLAGE—PARTNERSHIP PAYS

It is easy as a standard practice to rely on our own resources to recruit talent. But partnership pays. Partnering with other organizations, educational institutions, government entities, and local communities can yield effective strategies. There are two reasons why partnerships are important:

1. We are not just attracting talent but also the community to the company. Candidates are looking for a positive

experience, both in your workplace and in their lives. How much more powerful can your hiring and retention efforts be when the whole community is working with you?

2. Our resources are shrinking as a result of changing markets, competition, and regulatory pressures. Finding partners is a forward-thinking idea. All employers in an area need to attract talent and fill vacancies. Sharing resources may help alleviate financial strain while still filling vacancies.

This section outlines a few ways to partner with other entities.

Academic Partnerships

Academic partnerships are critical. Today there is a need to expand the number of university seats available for students and the types of academic programs to support different educational trends, such as accelerated degrees, night and weekend options, and "earn while you learn" programs. While academic institutions may struggle to fill their own faculty vacancies, it is a win if both healthcare and academic entities pull together, think outside the box, and develop new solutions.

State and Local Economic Development Partnerships

Hospitals are important economic drivers for communities. Healthcare drives economic growth through employment and the purchasing of goods and services. We are seeing healthcare organizations take a more proactive and participative role in economic development by addressing the social determinants of health, influencing affordable housing development, and supporting poverty reduction programs.

Healthcare organizations can also partner with economic development entities on talent development and attraction initiatives. Partnerships can yield increased training opportunities to enhance employees' skills, create new pipelines of qualified employees, align resources with critical needs, and develop strong relationships.

Community Training and Workforce Development Partnerships

When pursuing academic entities, don't forget about training and credentialing bodies. It is important to build strong relationships with training providers to open up access to licensing and credentialing exams. We have found these kinds of organizations to be quite open to collaborating on programs and expanding access to certification credentials.

Training entities may have the capacity to support upskilling or reskilling programs. They would make great partners for reaching out to underserved populations that may not have the means or ability to pursuing further education.

Partnerships are not a quick fix or one-time effort. To effectively leverage partnerships, you must have a mindset of developing strong and long-term relationships.

COMPETING WITH TRAVEL AND LOCUM AGENCIES

Travel and locum agencies are tough competitors for talent. But we need to see them as competitors to formulate an aggressive strategy. They are drawing your pool of nurses and physicians away, with promises of more money and the opportunity to travel.

Healthcare organizations do have grounds on which to compete, though. They can offer a safe place to call home. Compensation step-down or skill-up programs are benefits that agencies cannot provide. Contract buy-outs and flexible scheduling are also competitive options.

Patience and persistence are virtues in recruitment. Sometimes, agencies mess up and mishandle talent. We have heard stories of toxic management, nontransparent communication, and empty promises of bonuses or desired locations. If you have a strong and authentic culture at every location where you have travelers or locums, you could be the landing place for an otherwise disheartened professional.

KEEP IN TOUCH—THEY MAY COME BACK

Employees who leave but later come back are called boomerang employees. Often, boomerang employees are the best and most loyal workers after their return. They have may have found that the grass isn't greener on the other side of the fence. Or they may have picked up new skills and they are ready to put them to work at their original place of employment.

Given the value of a loyal, skilled employee, doesn't it make sense to maximize your ability to entice employees back to your organization? Savvy healthcare systems develop databases that allow them to stay in touch with employees after they leave. Using contact management applications, they can continue to celebrate milestones such as birthdays and provide updates on the organization and continuing education opportunities. They can also promote returning "home" with an offer of relocation and support.

YOUR OWN EMPLOYEES ARE YOUR BEST RECRUITERS

Your own employees can be your best recruiters, or they can torpedo your ability to attract talent. What employees say about your organization when leaders are not around matters.

In some cases, employees may not know how to handle a neighbor who is disappointed with a recent experience with your healthcare system. Others may feel their ambassadorship doesn't matter in the grand scheme of things. Still others may be disengaged and openly share their disappointment with working at your organization.

For example, a nurse in the Midwest expressed her concern that her hospital doesn't really care about its employees. She went on to say that many nurses who live locally would work anywhere else before even considering working for the hospital again. That is tragic, given the workforce shortage.

Get a handle on what your employees are saying about work when you are not around. What do you think they say to their neighbors or their family around the dinner table? Do you think they are comfortable recommending your organization as a good place to work to their friends and family? If not, you are missing a valuable opportunity to put solid horsepower into your recruiting strategy.

Consider equipping your employees to be ambassadors and to recruit new talent. A well-developed employee referral program goes beyond just bonuses for referring friends or family members. It also gives employees the tools and the opportunity to learn how to respond to bad press. Combined with a strong leadership team and culture, you may have a winning strategy that you have not yet tapped.

Preparing for the Future of Work

IN THE AFTERMATH of the COVID-19 pandemic, we are in largely uncharted territory. The global health crisis magnified challenges that are forcing organizations to rethink how they do business and how we define "normal." Those challenges will persist if we do not prepare for the future of work. Preparing proactively for workforce changes rather than merely reacting to them will be the difference between successful organizations and those that are left behind. As organizations approach the next strategic planning cycle, savvy leaders will put workforce shifts and trends on the agenda. This section provides a jumping-off point for your next strategic plan.

CHAPTER 9

How Macro-Level Shifts
Impact the Workforce

JUST WHEN YOU think you have it all figured out, everything changes. Smart leaders pay attention to macro-level shifts and how they affect workforce and the future of work.

If you want to attract and retain talented people, you must be able to identify and understand employee trends. Then you can respond and make changes to address those trends.

This chapter will speak to large, overall shifts: Geography, the local economy, work models, technology, and now the COVID-19 response all influence where employees choose to work. However, every organization will experience different impacts. You are encouraged to dig deep into your own workforce. Learn who your employees are and what makes them tick. When the world shakes and spins, you will know how your workforce will respond, and you will be there to guide them.

GENERATIONAL SHIFTS

Today's workforce is composed of five generations: Traditionalists, baby boomers, Generation X, millennials, and Generation Z. Undoubtedly you have already learned how each generation is different from the others. To get the most out of this book, however, you also need to understand how the generations are the same, and how each generation is changing the world of work in different ways. That understanding will help you develop a better strategy for leveraging employee strengths and influencing multi-generational engagement.

All generations want respect, safety, and security. Employees of all generations value fair career advancement opportunities. All generations want to work for a fair and consistent boss who has employees' backs—not just in lip service, but in action. Without those core principles in place, retention and recruitment will be a challenge regardless of generation.

These are a few ways that each generation influences the world of work:

- **Traditionalists**—also known as the "Silent Generation." Many have retired or are now working fewer hours. However, they still have influence in the workplace because of their experience and historical perspective.

- **Baby boomers**—considered workaholics with a strong work ethic. Retirements among boomers are expected to accelerate in the coming years. The loss of long-term knowledge and experience can be mitigated through talent management. Retaining these employees as long as possible is vital.

- **Generation X**—independent and skeptical. This generation introduced the idea of work–life balance. They have a strong work ethic and can see through ambiguity and confusion to prioritize solutions. They desire to perform meaningful work.

- **Millennials**—also known as Generation Y. They tend to crave new experiences. They work best as part of a team and require regular feedback. This generation can imagine workplace and customer experiences beyond the traditional status quo models.

- **Generation Z**—digitally savvy and well connected. This generation can be expected to advance technology far beyond our wildest dreams.

Of course, leaders should be careful to avoid stereotyping. We all have the ability and capacity to pick up strengths along the way that may be more prevalent in other generations. But understanding the unique concerns and strengths of each generation will help leaders develop a multigenerational leadership style.

TECHNOLOGY SHIFTS

There is an urgent need for tools to support a workforce that is already stretched thin. While technology alone cannot solve the workforce shortage, it can help leaders fill vacancies in a different way.

A technology-enabled care model has the potential to change future roles in healthcare delivery. Advances in robotics, healthcare facility design, and health informatics will continue to evolve and change the future of our work. For example, telemedicine has accelerated rapidly to allow healthcare providers to manage the health of our communities amid a pandemic.

Another example of technology at work was the establishment of command centers during the COVID-19 pandemic. These command centers utilized technology to move patients and resources across regions effectively and efficiently. Through the use of data analytics, monitoring capabilities, and communication platforms, these command centers helped health systems understand their reality.

Artificial intelligence (AI) can be used to communicate with large workforce groups and patients (e.g., using chatbots). AI technology is becoming more sophisticated, and our understanding of how to maximize it is in its infancy.

Technology enabled rapid transformation during the pandemic. For example, clinics were able to quickly transition from in-person care to remote or virtual visits to care for patients in the safety of their own homes.

Another innovation that the pandemic brought forward is the use of robots. Employing robots to deliver supplies so that human employees can be redeployed to other patient-facing work is not far from our reality.

During the pandemic, COVID-19 patients suffered from isolation behind closed doors, "no visitation" policies, and limited interactions with their nurses and physicians. Healthcare workers needed to find a way to provide human contact with these patients but also to monitor them from afar. Two technological tools, iPads and remote patient monitoring with two-way communication, were very useful during the pandemic. The iPads were used to connect patients and their families. Remote patient monitoring systems, which historically had been used as "telesitters," now allowed for observation of patients in isolation and remote verbal interactions with them. Best of all, patients could see a human face without a mask, shield, or hood.

COVID-19 MAGNIFIER: REDEPLOYMENT STRATEGIES

Some hospitals hard hit by the influx of COVID-19 patients found that traditional staffing models were inadequate. Healthcare leaders had no choice but to rethink their staffing models. They did so by redeploying existing staff to other locations, using more students than usual, reengaging retired healthcare professionals and activating travelers.

—*Tresha Moreland and Lori Wightman*

THE "NEW NORMAL"

Is there such a thing as "normal"? Was there ever a "normal"? Will things ever be "normal"? Our best advice for healthcare leaders is to get used to nothing being normal.

Setting aside structural and supply chain weakness discovered during the COVID-19 pandemic, the whole structure of healthcare is under close legislative and public scrutiny. Our industry is ripe for reinvention.

Research on disasters identifies six phases of a disaster and the ways in which people tend to respond during each phase.[1] To make a difference as healthcare leaders, we must understand these phases and be ready to meet the needs of our workforce at each phase. Consider how your organization responded during each phase of the COVID-19 pandemic. In retrospect, what would you have done differently before and during the pandemic? Is there anything you could do differently to prepare the workforce for a future disaster?

- **Phase 1.** The *pre-disaster phase* is characterized by fear and uncertainty.
- **Phase 2.** The *impact phase* is characterized by a range of intense emotional reactions. For example, during the pandemic, we observed panic buying of food and household supplies as a survival response.
- **Phase 3.** The *heroic phase* is characterized by a high level of activity and a low level of productivity. Early in the pandemic, we began to recognize who the heroes were—including, but not limited to, healthcare workers, grocery store workers, and delivery people.
- **Phase 4.** The *honeymoon phase* is characterized by a dramatic shift in emotion. Dips in case numbers and deaths brought about a new feeling of confidence.

- **Phase 5.** The *disillusionment phase* is characterized by discouragement and stress, replacing the optimism of the honeymoon phase. Surging case numbers in January 2021, for instance, left us feeling as if the pandemic would never end.
- **Phase 6.** The *reconstruction phase* is characterized by an overall feeling of recovery. Are we there yet?

Organizational leadership focused on building resilience and providing mental health support can help move the workforce through to the reconstruction phase.

NEW SUPPORT COMMUNITY WITHIN THE WORKPLACE

Over the past few decades, traditional support systems such as extended families, religious communities, and government institutions have lost influence, and the workplace has emerged as the primary domain where people seek to fulfill their social, spiritual, and economic needs. Organizations are seen as offering a sense of community and meaningful work beyond the salary. With that said, organizations need to take a more active role in employee support.

WORK MODELS

During the pandemic, most hospitals found that traditional staffing models were inadequate. Healthcare leaders had no choice but to rethink their staffing models and create an agile workforce. Some healthcare organizations are exploring and using alternative work models such as virtual, gig, or contract models. Today's workforce requires flexibility as part of the employee experience. Work models will continue to shift to meet the demand for more flexibility.

Clinical Work Models

Many healthcare organizations moved toward a team-based care model or similar collaborative care model. To stretch the expertise of nurses and physicians, teams were created in which experts were supported by nontraditional roles. Staff were cross-trained and redeployed to other departments or hospitals, students were used as part of the care teams, retired nurses were activated, and travelers were used. For example, at SCL Health in Colorado, the service excellence team worked with HR and incident command leaders to offer support groups, online mental health resources, and a community support resources directory for caregivers. The food service teams offered the purchase of milk, bread, and other basic groceries. In addition, they stocked frozen, ready-to-cook meals for caregivers to take home for their families. Finance and strategy employees became the data analytics team, creating needed dashboards for monitoring the impact of COVID-19.

Nonclinical Work Models

Before the pandemic, leaders were reluctant to adopt a work-from-home model, concerned about the ability to maintain productivity. The pandemic forced the issue, however, and sending people home to work was the only way to keep employees safe and comply with lockdowns. There is growing evidence to refute the idea that remote employees are not productive. In fact, many organizations have found that employees may be more productive working at home. However, leaders may be concerned about the impact of remote work on organizational culture. Now we must answer a new set of questions: What is the long-term remote strategy? Will this be the new norm? Will we continue to have a portion of the healthcare workforce working remotely? It is likely that many organizations will adopt a hybrid model that encourages a combination of remote and in-person work.

COVID-19 MAGNIFIER: KEY WORKFORCE LESSONS FROM THE COVID-19 PANDEMIC

Large shifts are occurring within the workforce, but we have also observed "micro-shifts" that are having a large impact. The following list details critical factors that required consistent attention throughout the pandemic and must be monitored going forward.

- **Emergency management structure.** How is it holding up during a long-term crisis? What have we learned? What improvements can be made to prepare for future crises? Consider emergency management training for all levels of leadership in your organization.

- **Surge planning.** We will see surges in patient volume that extend beyond a hospital's capability again. In the event of patient volume surges, collaboration with other health systems across a city, region, or state is critical and must be an ongoing effort.

- **Communication.** Effective crisis communication must be clear, frequent, and authentic. Step up by being truthful, sincere, and compassionate. Ensure that your communications are delivered using a variety of methods—in person, in writing, and virtual. Consider the diversity of your workforce. Are you communicating at a level that all employees can understand? Are you providing communications in different languages to support employees who do not speak English as their first language?

- **Collaboration.** Internal collaboration must occur at all levels of the organization and between teams

(continued)

(continued from previous page)

that may have not worked together before. Consider how to prepare for this kind of intense, unique collaboration by training employees in areas such as safety culture, effective team communication, and leadership.

- **Workforce stabilization.** The pandemic rocked an already unstable healthcare workforce. The demand for travel and temporary clinical staff exceeded the labor pool available, driving wages for temporary staff sky high. The opportunity to make exceptionally high wages, even for a short period, pulled clinical staff out of organizations when they were needed the most. Organizations must evaluate their care delivery models, compensation programs, and retention strategies to create a sustainable future.

- **Mind, body, and spirit of the workforce.** The pandemic created a workforce marked by signs of grief, moral distress, burnout, and even post-traumatic stress disorder. This impact is evident in increasing turnover since the pandemic. Employees are choosing to leave the profession, retire early, take positions outside of acute care, or move to part-time status. Additionally, employee illness, leaves of absence, and loss of productivity are impacting healthcare organizations. What steps is your organization taking to restore the workforce?

—Tresha Moreland and Lori Wightman

WORKFORCE STRATEGIES TO ADDRESS
CRITICAL MICRO-LEVEL SHIFTS

A group of chief nurse executives in Colorado worked together to develop guiding principles for care delivery and the workforce during the pandemic. They wanted to balance the needs of all patients in the communities they serve. Recognizing that staffing healthcare organizations during a pandemic is a dynamic process, they found it helpful to make decisions based on a few guiding principles that might be helpful in navigating micro-level shifts. These principles include the following:

- Decisions will be based on organizational mission, vision, and values, as well as ethical principles.
- Decisions about workforce staffing and patient care delivery will be made by clinical leaders with input from frontline caregivers.
- Nurse workload will be evaluated and adjusted to meet the demands of the community; patient acuity will be considered.
- Alternative models of care will be employed as needed to meet the care needs of the community. The strategies include, but are not limited to,
  - Upskilling and cross-training of clinical and nonclinical staff to create agility in the workforce (e.g., utilization of clinical students, EMTs, LPNs, and other support roles to complete care teams)
  - Seeking the support of retired workers to reengage in patient care
  - Redeploying clinical employees to serve as helping hands or part of a care team
  - Redeploying nonclinical employees to function in support roles (e.g., runners, unit clerks, stocking, screening, transport)

- Assigning clinical leaders to care for patients and/or serve on a care team
- "Travel" clinical and nonclinical staff will be utilized to supplement the current workforce, even though the national demand for travel staff is extremely high and difficult to secure.
- Workforce mind, body, and spirit will be monitored and strategies implemented to promote resilience, health, and well-being.
- Clinical employees may be redeployed within a health system.
- Clinical employees may be shared across health systems.
- Federal and state assistance may be needed to meet patient care demand.
- Caregivers will be cared for by conducting regular crisis debriefings and implementing programs to support them personally and professionally during and after the crisis.

POLITICAL SHIFTS

In the coming years, we can expect to see renewed calls for a "Medicare for All" or universal healthcare model. Under such a plan, the government would provide all aspects of healthcare, including paying for healthcare, employing providers, and running facilities. The veterans healthcare system is an example of this model.

We can also expect an increase in employment regulations, such as the adoption of aggressive labor unionization policies that could include the elimination of "right to work" states, an increase in the overtime threshold (implemented during the Barack Obama administration), an increase in the federal minimum wage, a ban on individual arbitration agreements, additional standards for classifying independent contractors, and increased employer oversight by government agencies.

Regardless of the changes we face in healthcare, as leaders, we must accomplish the following:

- Apply key lessons from the COVID-19 pandemic: communication, collaboration, innovation, application of technology, and creative yet supportive workforce strategies.
- Ensure that patients and their families remain at the center of decision-making.
- Support the healthcare workforce through crisis and a period of restoration, taking into full consideration the mind, body, and spirit of employees.
- Ensure that safe, quality patient care is accessible across the care continuum.
- Deliver healthcare in a way that is equitable and honors diversity.

NOTE

1. DeWolfe, D. J. 2000. *Training Manual for Mental Health and Human Service Workers in Major Disasters*, 2nd ed. US Department of Health and Human Services, Substance Abuse and Mental Health Services Administration. Accessed March 22, 2021. www.hsdl.org/?view&did=4017.

CHAPTER 10

Pulling the Future into the Present

WE CAN PREDICT the future. We can understand the workforce and monitor the environment to see what is coming and how it may affect our ability to attract and retain staff. This chapter will discuss workforce planning and how to leverage what we learn from it to help our organizations recruit and retain staff. (For a detailed Strategic Workforce Planning Checklist, see appendix F.)

LOOK INTO THE FUTURE THROUGH WORKFORCE PLANNING

Strategic workforce planning is a formal process that proactively anticipates current and future hiring needs. This is done through the use of business, finance, and HR analytics and leadership insight. It also includes monitoring external influences such as the environment, competition, and geographical changes, as described in chapter 9.

One such external influence is migration patterns. Before the COVID-19 pandemic, we were already observing out-migration from metropolitan areas. Although overall migration patterns slowed during the pandemic, we observed that the hardest-hit metropolitan areas with restrictive lockdown measures, such as

New York City and San Francisco, saw an acceleration of out-migration. Identifying external trends like migration patterns can help healthcare leaders craft and apply smart recruitment strategies. For example, some rural areas became attractive places to live and work because of their larger homes, spacious yards, and ease of social distancing. Organizations in rural markets may target prospective employees in metropolitan areas and promote their location as a safe place to live.

WORKFORCE PLANNING SAVES A SERVICE LINE

After yet another retirement request came through my office, I started to get curious. This was half a dozen retirements over the course of 30 days. I decided to investigate how many of our employees will be within retirement age, and when might they be expected to retire?

My analysis uncovered something shocking: *all* of our nuclear medicine technologists were going to be within retirement age in the next two years.

"Oh yes, they all started at the same time, became friends, and are talking about retiring at the same time. They attend each other's family reunions and are very excited about it. I hadn't really thought about what that meant, though," explained the director.

We worked together to plan a talent pipeline strategy that we could implement immediately. Had we not proactively learned this fact about our workforce, an entire service line would have been wiped out until staff could be recruited.

—*Tresha Moreland*

NO SURPRISES: PREPARE FOR THE UNEXPECTED

By now, most of us are feeling burned from "surprises." If you weren't before, surely the pandemic has you there now. We don't like surprises anymore! But surprises are a fact of life; therefore, the best question to ask is, how can we better prepare for the unexpected?

This is where scenario planning comes into play. Asking "what if" questions is paramount for the healthcare industry, where it seems anything can happen. Brainstorming all possibilities, no matter how wild they might seem, is a good practice. You can do two things with this list.

1. Start small by narrowing the list down to the most likely scenarios. Then develop a plan to address a few likely scenarios.
2. Go big and apply indicators (we call them "tripwires") to all of the scenarios and monitor them. If a tripwire (or more than one) is triggered, activate your contingency plan(s). This approach would enable a more agile organization to respond effectively.

OPTIMIZE THE WORKFORCE

What does productivity mean to you? Does it mean how fast you can get through your never-ending stream of emails? Does it mean being prompt to every meeting? Or does it mean that you are good at multitasking? These factors may be a part of productivity, but healthcare executives must consider a larger picture in today's business reality.

Labor costs are typically the highest expense for any healthcare organizations. Studies show the largest investment, in people, has a direct correlation with customer satisfaction, quality, and revenue.

It's no wonder that optimizing the workforce is something that highly service-oriented organizations pursue.

It's easy to get lost in the concept of workforce optimization. Many leaders do not really understand how workforce optimization works. Leaders who chase workforce optimization without understanding it tend to spend a lot of time focusing on a particular metric or figuring out how to encourage employees to work harder, only to find that they are spinning their wheels. Workforce optimization goes beyond productivity metrics. Highly productive organizations have learned that true workforce optimization requires a sustained focus on multiple fronts.

Workforce optimization is focused on balancing customer needs, service levels, workforce scheduling, service workflows, and operational costs to get the maximum benefit from employees at any given time. It's not just about efficiency. It's about effectiveness, too. It's about finding the right resource, at the right time, at the right cost, to yield the right results.

By following these steps, you can make the most of your workforce optimization efforts:

- **Define your value.** If your only goal is to determine staffing levels and save money, then you might want to revisit the definition of workforce optimization. Indeed, market pressures create an urgent need to reduce labor expenses. But the definition of value is service at the lowest cost for the highest quality. True workforce optimization is a means toward that end. If the patient is left out of the effort, then you've lost the game from the beginning.
- **Patients come first.** Take a patient-first approach. Analyze and identify breakdowns in providing optimal customer service. Consider department workflows, employee skill sets, and resource needs. Then, look at staffing levels and time wasted on non-value-added activities that do not benefit the customer. For example, a healthcare

organization could study non-value-added activities that prevent nurses from spending time with patients. You might have to reengineer care delivery, business processes, and scheduling practices to ensure you are getting the right result. But remember, workforce optimization is about ensuring the right staff, in the right place, with the right results is occurring, every time, every day.

- **Leverage labor effectiveness.** Effectiveness of your workforce is not about having the right number of FTEs or how much you are spending on overtime. It's also about determining whether you have the right kind of FTEs to perform the work necessary. Ask yourself these questions about your labor effectiveness:

  - What are the scheduling practices throughout the system? Are scheduling standards clearly defined and communicated? Or is it "anything goes"?

  - Do you have the right skill and job mix performing the right tasks? Are licensed employees working at the top of their licensure?

  - Do you have the right staffing mix of full-time, part-time, and per diem staff to meet your patient volume?

  - Do you have the right span of control and management scope?

- **Engage your employees.** Monitor employee engagement levels as part of your workforce optimization efforts. Who better to identify new, innovative ways to deliver services than the individuals performing the work!

- **Continuously monitor progress.** Don't fall into the trap of taking your eye off the ball when your immediate goals are met. "FTE creep" or "drift" from workflows and standard practices can happen if standards are not enforced over time, leading to disaster for the organization.

By implementing a "work smarter, not harder" concept, employees will be able to endure "doing more with less," and burnout will be less likely. When considering productivity and human resources, look beyond the question of how fast we can complete processes. Evaluate productivity at a higher level, so that patient, employee, and financial gains can be realized.

USE PEOPLE ANALYTICS TO DRIVE CHANGE

More than 20 years ago, the notion of using "people measures" was considered impossible. However, people analytics have come a long way—thankfully! Today, people analytics don't just measure the past, but also the present and future.

We have observed a lot of confusion about people analytics in many organizations. Organizations may make the mistake of choosing a lot of measures to monitor, just to have something to measure and report to executives or the board. However, unless those measures are gauging behavioral or organizational changes, the effort is wasted.

Effective metrics have the following ten traits. Take a look at this list and compare your metrics against these standards.

1. **Strategic metrics.** If a measure is not connected to an organizational objective, vision, or mission, it's not strategic. A good strategic metric helps leaders monitor whether the organization is on track to achieve its goals. Anything else is just a number. At worst, poor metrics could distract leaders from achieving real results.

2. **Actionable**. Metrics should be tied to a particular action. For example, if a measure is trending downward, the organization's leaders and employees should know what to do to get back on track. It's no use spending time measuring activities if no one can affect the outcome.

3. **Accurate.** Metrics should be accurate—otherwise, they lose all creditability. To go a step further, metrics should also be validated. Validating metrics can and should test your hypothesis. For example, an organization may wish to measure something that is self-reported by leaders. However, we know that self-reported data are subject to bias or human errors. Validating metrics and the hypotheses they are based on will ensure that the numbers are meaningful and the assumptions underlying them are sound.

4. **Standardized and (when possible) evidence-based.** Effective metrics should be standardized. Current evidence or best practices should be evaluated as internal metrics are established. Leaders should agree on the definition of each measure, the scope of the measure, the frequency of the measurement report out, and so on. This agreement should occur up front—not after a measure has been launched that could make or break a key organizational objective.

5. **Timely.** People in finance know this better than anyone. What is the use of reporting on financial measures several months after a period closes? By that time, it's too late to act if something has gone awry. Timely metrics enable the organization to act fast when something requires attention.

6. **Bigger picture.** Workforce optimization has moved beyond a single focus on productivity. Patient acuity, patient placement, staffing models, and workforce agility all come into focus now.

7. **Dedicated commitment.** To keep an eye on analytics, consider establishing a formal role in the organization, such as a system director of nursing workforce optimization. This full-time job would be a labor management position that includes overseeing staffing

models, policies and practices, agency management, budgeting, and so on.

8. **Remember the whole ship.** Move beyond a focus on nursing labor. To be sure, nursing labor is the largest expense in an acute care workforce, but other departments also contribute to the direction of the ship. Replicate workforce analytics and monitoring in non-nursing operations areas as well. Effectiveness and efficiency should be consistent across the enterprise.

9. **True purpose.** Workforce management is all about culture change. Leaders must be competent in change management and knowledgeable about the organization's culture.

10. **Engagement.** Engagement of the people doing the work is vital to success.

High performance requires utilizing the right metrics, the right way. Start shining a light on your measures. If you are foggy, that light will clear the way to authentic action and high-impact performance in the future.

Conclusion

FACING THE HEALTHCARE workforce shortage is a daunting task that is not for the faint of heart. Certainly, the COVID-19 pandemic created instability and complexities. Coping with these challenges will require a stomach for authentic and sincere reinvention of our existing approaches. We can't say there is a magic pill or quick fix that will solve the workforce shortage. Nor can we say that anyone has all the answers. There is a lot of work to be done!

But by applying creative thinking, resourcefulness, and an authentic commitment to doing the heavy lifting, over time, vacancies can be filled and valuable employees retained. Throughout this book, we have taken a fresh look at these critical components:

- Organizational resilience
- Organizational culture
- Retention
- Employee engagement
- Organizational alignment
- Strategic collective bargaining
- Internal recruitment
- External recruitment
- Workforce shifts
- Workforce forecasting and planning

Healthcare executives have an ongoing obligation to ensure safe, quality care for the communities they serve. We want to help beyond the pages of this book. What is your organization doing to stabilize and rebuild the healthcare workforce? We would love to hear from you! It will take many innovative strategies to ensure a stable workforce—we want to know what other ideas we may have missed.

Contact us at Tresha@hrcsuite.com.

Tools and Checklists

Pre-work Checklist

THE FOLLOWING TEN-STEP process will help prepare your organization and build the strength and resilience necessary to successfully navigate challenges, abrupt shifts in direction, and crises.

STEP 1: DO YOUR PERSONAL "PRE-WORK"

- Do you take time to rest, deactivate, and replenish your energy in healthy ways?
- Do you engage in activities that promote expansion of your knowledge, thinking, skills, and awareness?
- Do you create time and space for quiet reflection through meditation, prayer, or journaling?
- Do you exercise and eat nutritious foods?
- Do you get enough sleep?
- Do you set healthy boundaries on your work hours?

STEP 2: DEVELOP A RESILIENT WORKFORCE

Employees

- Is employee engagement in your organization about the employee engagement survey score, or about the people?
- Do your employees exhibit these resilient characteristics?
    - They have a strong support system to help manage stress and burnout.
    - They have passion and perseverance to run a marathon rather than just a sprint.
    - They have mental toughness and flexibility to bounce back from difficult situations and setbacks.
    - They resist getting involved in unnecessary drama and avoid negative people who drag them down.

Leaders

- Are your leaders aligned with the organization's mission and values?
- Do your leaders lead with their head only, or also with their heart?
- Which leadership style is pervasive in your organization—command and control, leadership by lip service, or authentic heart-driven leadership?
- Are your leaders engaged?
- Are leaders also taking care of their mind, body and spirit?

Mission and Values

- Do you hire people who are aligned with the organization's mission and values?

- Do your leaders resist convenience hiring and take the time to hire individuals who are aligned with the organization's mission and vision?

STEP 3: DEVELOP AUTHENTIC RELATIONSHIPS

- Do you know what authentic relationships look like? Do your leaders know?
- Are you using a framework of relationship-based care (relationship with self, relationship with colleagues, relationship with patients and families)?
- Does your leadership team (all team members) make it safe to share information and ideas without fear?
- Rate your relationships with the following stakeholders:

  A. Employees
    - Do your employees know and trust the organization's leadership *before* a crisis occurs?
    - Are there divisions between departments or workgroups?
    - Does the organization have a cultural expectation of teamwork, care, and compassion for colleagues?

  B. Leaders
    - Do your leaders embrace the importance of trust and respect?
    - Do your leaders work hard at developing healthy working relationships?
    - Do your leaders have a "one for all" approach and no "turf" building?
    - Do your leaders possess grace and assume good intentions?

  C. Customers
    - Is it clear who the organization's customers are?

- Who are the internal customers?
- Who are the external customers?
- Are employed or affiliated physicians treated as customers?
- Do your relationships with patients and families go beyond chasing patient experience survey scores?
  - Do you meet their "hotel" expectations, or are you just a lifeline to the patient?
  - How did you manage the impact of "no visitors" during the pandemic?
  - How is your relationship with the community (or communities) you serve?
  - Does the community value and respect its community hospital and physician practices?

D. Partners

- How have you been developing partnerships with government officials? Advocacy work can help government officials understand healthcare and the challenges we face.
- Do you view your partnerships with vendors and representatives from supply companies as partners?
- How is your organization's relationship with the manufacturers that supply products you use to serve patients?
- How are your relationships with other healthcare organizations?

STEP 4: COMMUNICATE STRATEGICALLY AND EFFECTIVELY

- Are your communication themes aligned with core organizational values?

- Is the tone of organizational communication authentic?
- Do your communication messages get to all employees, including frontline employees?
- Do employees hear your key messages *before* they hear them on the evening news?
- Are your leaders regularly visible to employees *before* a crisis (e.g., rounding, town halls, staff meetings)?

STEP 5: DEVELOP LEADERS AT ALL LEVELS OF THE ORGANIZATION

- Are your leadership development initiatives available to all leaders, including frontline leaders?
- Are your safety training and drills engaging and frequent?
- Do you cross-train employees?
- Do you have a method for redeploying staff to other areas of the organization? Do you sponsor and develop leaders by exposing them to different experiences?
- Do you use techniques such as coaching and mentorship to support ongoing learning?
- Do you have a long-term virtual learning strategy?

STEP 6: INVEST IN TECHNOLOGY PLATFORMS THAT CAN ADAPT QUICKLY

- What are your short- and long-term strategies for remote care and remote work?
- Does your existing technology support those strategies?
- Do you have the optimal management of staffing needs per floor and per shift?

- Can you efficiently distribute specialty talent where it's needed?
- Are you maximizing the existing talent you have available?
- Are staff working at the top of their license (i.e., can you free them to work on higher-level care activities)?
- Are you building and developing existing staff to perform needed roles?
- Are you analyzing and predicting turnover?
- How do you enable smart and responsive candidate recruitment communication?
- Are you using smart people analytics?

STEP 7: REFRESH YOUR EMERGENCY MANAGEMENT TRAINING AND TEAM

- Do you have a response structure in place, and are you reviewing it periodically?
- Do you train leaders at all levels on emergency management principles and roles?
- Do you have in-house emergency management experts?
- Are drills taken seriously by all levels of leadership? Really?
- Do you regularly engage in scenario planning?
- Does your emergency management program account for multiple scenarios?
- Have you applied what you learned from the COVID-19 pandemic to enhance your emergency management protocols?
- Are you leveraging relationships with other healthcare systems, medical groups, and the community?

STEP 8: EVALUATE FINANCIAL STEWARDSHIP

- Do you have a strategy ready in the event of financial strain?
- Is the organization good at flexing to service demand, beyond the clinical staff?
- Do employees at all levels of the organization understand their part in financial stewardship and why it is important?
- Do you have a workforce optimization strategy?
- Does the organization have a financial stewardship position in place *before* a crisis?

STEP 9: MAINTAIN SAFE AND HIGH-QUALITY SERVICES

- What communication strategies will be effective with a fearful and distrustful population?
- Does your organization have a reputation for safe and quality care? What are you doing beyond branding messages to improve your reputation?
- What do your employees say at the dinner table and to neighbors about your safety and quality practices? Are your employees your reputation ambassadors or assassins?
- Do you ensure quality of care through a solid cross-training program?
- Have you prepared business office staff to support patient care?
- How transparent is your data for employees and the community?

STEP 10: CREATE A CULTURE OF INNOVATION

- What steps are you taking to shape a culture of innovation and creativity?
- Are your frontline employees actively engaged in process improvement, workflow redesign, and development of solutions?
- Is it safe for employees to solve problems, fail, and try again?
- Do you embrace different thinking and ideas? Do you avoid like-minded, groupthink, yes people?

Organizational Culture Assessment Checklist

Use this checklist to get a better understanding of how to assess and repair or enhance an already strong organizational culture. Instead of trying to do everything at once, consider prioritizing action items that can create quick wins.

MISSION, VISION, AND VALUES: ROAD MAP TO SUCCESS

- Does your organization have a mission, vision, and values?
- If so, how relevant are they today?
- Are your employees aware of them?
- Do your leaders consistently model these priorities?
- Do your core values have to compete for attention with pillars, objectives, and branding messages?

HIRING: CULTURE ALIGNMENT

- Do you hire employees and leaders who share your organization's vision and values?

- Do you hire people who can strengthen your culture (e.g., people who challenge the status quo and have the courage to speak up, as opposed to those who think alike or go with the flow)?

ONBOARDING: SET THE TONE

- Do you orient employees to your organizational culture in addition to policies and procedures?
- Does your orientation to organizational culture start before the first day of employment (e.g., manager and team welcome messages, passport to success)?

LEADERS WALKING THE TALK: EMPLOYEES SEE THE TRUTH IN LEADER ACTIONS

- Do your leaders model behaviors that are aligned with your stated values?
- Do you keep leaders who model and find a different path for those who don't (e.g., are there rewards or consequences for leaders who do or don't model organizational values)?
- Do you foster transparency (e.g., is it safe to be open and honest in meetings)?
- Do you encourage open communication among all levels of your organization (e.g., leaders rounding, greeting employees, asking for honest feedback, following up with and getting back to employees with answers to their questions)?
- Do your leaders demonstrate through their actions that they value collaboration and teamwork (e.g., as opposed to positioning for power, backstabbing, engaging in negative behaviors)?

PERFORMANCE MANAGEMENT

- Do your values guide your performance management activities (e.g., does the performance assessment process evaluate core values)?
- Does your performance management process help employees improve (e.g., rather than rubber-stamping evaluation forms year after year)?
- Is the importance of your core values emphasized in meetings, town hall meetings, etc.?

REWARDS AND RECOGNITION

- Do bonuses help foster a strong culture? Take an inventory of all your bonus programs and evaluate whether they support a strong culture or inadvertently undermine a desired culture.
- Do you recognize and thank those who model behaviors that are aligned with core organizational values (e.g., do annual employee banquets only celebrate years of service, or do they also recognize culture heroes)?

METRICS: EFFECTIVE MONITORING TRULY MAKES A DIFFERENCE

- Are your current channels of communication effective? Do those channels help or hinder employees in sending, receiving, and understanding information?
- Of all the metrics you measure, do any indicate how the components of the organization are aligned with core values?
- Do you have metrics to measure how effectively and efficiently new ideas are vetted?

- Do you have measures that indicate whether employees feel supported by the organization, their supervisors, their coworkers, and leadership?
- Are you measuring employees' feelings about trust?
- Are you measuring teamwork as well as cross-functional teams (e.g., how well do members of the marketing department work among themselves and with other departments)?

Employee Experience Journey Template

	Recruitment and Onboarding Experience	Employment Experience	Offboarding Experience
Process	How easy is it to navigate organizational processes? Are they mobile-friendly and convenient, or frustrating and inconvenient?	What is the experience of changing an address, enrolling in new benefits, or inquiring about some aspect of employment?	What is the experience of resigning or retiring?
Tools and technology	How quickly do new employees receive computer access and the tools necessary to do their jobs? Is this process streamlined or disjointed?	Do you provide ongoing support for technology and tools?	Do you have the capability to stay in touch with former employees, and vice versa?
People	How well does your onboarding approach help new employees develop relationships?	How are relationships with coworkers and supervisors? Are connections strong or broken?	Are relationships strong enough that former employees would feel welcome to return?

(continued)

	Recruitment and Onboarding Experience	Employment Experience	Offboarding Experience
Moments that matter	How memorable is your onboarding experience?	How do you acknowledge and recognize moments that matter?	Is your exit process memorable and warm? Would former employees want to come back to the organization?
Communication	How effective is your communication? Does the job meet expectations? Are employees getting all the important information they need?	How well do you keep employees informed and involved?	Does your communication approach keep former employees connected with your organization?
Opportunities	What opportunities for improvement exist?	What opportunities for improvement exist?	What opportunities for improvement exist?

Recruitment and Onboarding Experience

Process	• Job posting • Outreach • Application • Job offer	• New hire onboarding, orientation • Enrolling in benefits • Obtaining tools and access to technology • Learning about organization, role, expectations, goals	• Connecting and developing relationships • Meeting and greeting
Define the ideal experience			
What is the actual experience and why?			

	Recruitment and Onboarding Experience	Employment Experience	Offboarding Experience
Employment Experience			
Process	• Performance feedback • Recognition and acknowledgment • Convenient options for managing benefits and compensation • Flexibility in scheduling • Communication of internal updates versus news headlines	• Learning and development options • Career advancement opportunities • Internal mobility options (transfers) • Participation in projects and new initiatives	• Ongoing relationships with coworkers and supervisors • Inclusive environment • Civil environment • Ability to connect with others
Define the ideal experience			
What is the actual experience and why?			
Offboarding Experience			
Process	• Does the exit process maintain the employee's dignity, or is it a painful process? • What is the process like for termination or resignation versus retirement?	• Is the information shared with employees current and accurate? • Are employees informed about how to return?	• Communication mechanism for keeping in touch • Alumni group connections • Return-to-work updates

(continued)

Define the ideal experience	
What is the actual experience and why?	

Organizational Alignment Assessment Checklist

DIAGNOSING MISALIGNMENT

Symptoms of a misaligned organization include the following:

- Executives think in terms of the organizational chart (boxes and lines) and not system alignment.
- Leaders do not have the same focus or the same agenda.
- Organizational design is left to chance and to the inexperienced.
- Activities are mistaken as results or progress—much like tactics are mistaken for strategy.
- Complexity rules the day—confusion and disputes abound because of a lack of clarity on roles and responsibilities.
- There are too many meetings and not enough time to execute strategy.
- Communication and strategy development occur in silos—everyone is serving their own interests or those of their team.
- Decision-making takes too long.

STEPS TO REALIGNMENT

- Organizational direction—"Level set" everyone's understanding of the overall direction. Make sure events, meetings, and projects are lined up with the overall direction.

- Organizational structure—Who is responsible for what? Which skills are necessary and which are lacking? What processes need to be integrated, fixed, or banished? Dump the existing organizational chart. List key deliverables that the organization must accomplish, and then right next to those deliverables, which leaders and departments are directly responsible for them.

- Management execution—Establish measures and short- and mid-range objectives and ensure the leadership team is executing toward them.

- Budgets and rewards—Are resources allocated to the right priorities? Are people being rewarded for the right priorities (e.g., providing exceptional care versus just showing up to work)?

- Communication—Do you authentically cascade the vision, purpose, and direction to all levels of the organization? Does your communication take the right tone at all times? Do your mid-level and frontline leaders actively communicate key messages to staff?

Recruitment Effectiveness
Assessment Checklist

Use the assessment on pages 146–48 to diagnose and optimize your recruitment efforts. Don't fret if you answer "no" to many of these questions. This assessment is intended to challenge and inspire you to raise the bar of service delivery.

Description	Yes	No	Notes
Planning and Strategy			
Does the organization invest in and support recruitment?			
Are future workplace needs factored into planning?			
Are labor market trends factored into planning?			
Are talent strategies linked to business strategies?			
Does the organization leverage data-driven insights?			
Workforce Planning and Segmentation			
Has the organization identified ideal job skills, experiences, and competencies?			
Has the organization identified skill gaps?			
Does the organization take a predictive approach to talent management and recruitment (i.e., understanding turnover trends and implementing strategies to mitigate vacancy timelines)?			
Does the organization use a specific recruitment approach for each targeted audience?			

Employer Branding

Has the organization defined its employer brand and made it a key element of talent acquisition?

Are job descriptions and posts accurate and appealing?

Can job candidates find out what it's like to work for your company online?

Does the organization have a favorable reputation online (e.g., Glassdoor.com, Indeed.com)?

Is the employer brand linked to the organization's brand?

Talent Sourcing

Is the organization constantly seeking new sources of talent?

Is the organization open to seeking diverse pools of talent?

Do you live where your candidates live (e.g., visit conferences, professional forums, social media networks; acquainted with target audience speakers)?

Does the organization have an effective employee referral program?

Talent Relationship Management

Is there a strong partnership with hiring managers?

Do hiring managers have frequent and consistent interactions with candidates?

Does the organization have the capacity to develop connections rather than just numbers?

(continued)

Description	Yes	No	Notes
Measures for Success			
Does the organization use metrics to monitor effectiveness, efficiency, and impact?			
Examples:			
Cost per hire (efficiency)			
Quality per hire (effectiveness)			
Vacancy rate (impact)			
Candidate net promoter score (effectiveness and impact)			
Sourcing channel effectiveness (effectiveness)			
Applicant to open position ratio (effectiveness)			
Time to fill (efficiency)			
Offer acceptance rate (impact)			

Strategic Workforce Planning Checklist

STEP 1: INTRODUCTION

- What are the organization's vision, mission, and goals/objectives?
- What are the organization's core business functions?
- Do you anticipate any changes to the organization's structure or business delivery model (e.g., new service lines, new products, structural changes such as providing more services online)? What does the organization's future look like?

STEP 2: DEMAND ANALYSIS

- What are the internal and external workforce trends and influences?
  - Internal: Are there internal workforce trends, such as increasing retirements or increasing or decreasing turnover?
  - External: Are there environmental, political, regulatory, market changes that will influence how the organization operates in the future? In what ways?

STEP 3: SUPPLY ANALYSIS

- Does the organization currently have enough employees?
- Do current employees have the knowledge, skills, and abilities needed to address critical business issues in the future?

STEP 4: GAP ANALYSIS

- What shortages or surpluses in staffing and skill levels can you identify?
- What impact will retirement and turnover trends have in the future?
- Will the organization have the employees and skill sets to accomplish its goals in the future?

STEP 5: BUILD WORKFORCE PLAN(S)

- What are your recommendations for resolving gaps (e.g., changes in organizational structure, succession planning, retention programs, recruitment plans, career development, leadership development programs, employee development)?

Index

About the Authors

 **Tresha Moreland, FACHE, MBA, MS, SPHR,** is a business adviser and executive who helps those who are serious about raising the bar of excellence to achieve their organization's objectives. She has held key human resources leadership roles for more than 30 years in industries such as manufacturing, distribution, retail, hospitality, and healthcare.

Tresha holds master's degrees in human resources management and business administration. She also earned certifications as a Senior Professional in Human Resources and as a Six Sigma Black Belt Professional. She is a fellow of the American College of Healthcare Executives.

Tresha's specialties as an executive and principal consultant include organizational strategic planning, workforce planning, talent pipeline planning, talent management/employee engagement, leadership development and succession planning, business transition facilitation (mergers/acquisitions, restructures, joint ventures, shared services), workforce productivity implementation and management, and internal communication.

Lori Wightman, MSN, DNP, RN, NEA-BC, enjoyed providing hands-on care to patients in the intensive care setting. She obtained her master's degree in nursing to serve patients as a clinical nurse specialist. However, once she fell into her first leadership position, she realized that she could have a greater impact on patients and their families as a leader in support of caregivers in healthcare. Now she is a doctoral-prepared chief nursing officer with more than 25 years of progressive nursing leadership experience in diverse healthcare settings.

Lori's personal mission is to develop nurses and leaders capable of transforming care. She developed coaching skills through the Blue Mesa executive coaching program. In addition, her doctoral work centered on succession planning, coaching, and mentoring leaders. She has served as faculty in university nursing programs to contribute to the growth of the profession.